Arnold Schoenberg

by Bojan Bujić

Phaidon Press Limited
Regent's Wharf
All Saints Street
London N1 9PA

Phaidon Press Inc.
180 Varick Street
New York, NY 10014

www.phaidon.com

First published 2011
© 2011 Phaidon Press Limited

ISBN 978 0 7148 4614 9

A CIP catalogue record for this book is
available from the British Library.

Designed by HDR Visual Communication

Printed in China

Frontispiece,
Arnold Schoenberg
conducting the Los Angeles
Federal Music Project
Symphony Orchestra,
March 1937.

Contents

Preface

An encyclopedia biography of Arnold Schoenberg might dispassionately begin as follows: 'Austrian-born composer, music theorist, composition teacher, critic, poet, essayist, painter, philosopher, political activist and inventor.' This book aims to elucidate and set in its cultural context the immensely rich life of a composer who is, arguably, the central musical personality of the twentieth century. There is much debate as to whether Schoenberg is the greatest composer of his time – although his innovative musical language opened up new possibilities for composers, it did not appeal to all of those who came after him. But, directly or indirectly, he affected so many musicians and listeners of his own and of subsequent generations that his significance cannot be disputed. Some people argue that Schoenberg's uncompromising search for an individual voice led him to create music that is too difficult to follow, since many of the familiar features that normally enable listeners to find their way through a piece have been removed or radically reshaped. This in turn was perceived as the main cause of the isolation of avant-garde music in the late twentieth century. The trouble is that these accusations are frequently made before Schoenberg's music has even had a chance to be heard – its perceived difficulty and strangeness often become a barrier that prevents the music from being appreciated in its own right. Schoenberg's enormous importance as a theorist of tonal music is more readily accepted, and the theory of twelve-note music, developed after Schoenberg, readily finds a wide readership among music students. This creates the danger that Schoenberg the theorist may become discussed more widely than Schoenberg the composer is listened to.

There is no 'typical' Schoenberg. It is important not to fall for the commercially inspired notion that listening should be 'easy', and so limit one's experience to his more approachable works such as the sextet *Verklärte Nacht* or the oratorio *Gurrelieder*. Schoenberg's orchestral and chamber music is richly rewarding; *Pierrot lunaire*, the

Serenade, Op. 24 and Suite, Op. 29 offer fascinating constructions in sound, while the choral works, from the early *Friede auf Erden* to the late *De profundis*, carry some of the most haunting choral sounds of the twentieth century. If this book succeeds in encouraging more people to listen to Schoenberg's music, its aim will have been more than achieved.

I first became aware of Schoenberg in the 1950s, as an undergraduate in Yugoslavia, when Miroslav Spiller, who had been his student in Berlin, led me through the labyrinths of the analysis of tonal music. Spiller was not at all sympathetic to the twelve-note method, but this only spurred me on to find out more about this aspect of Schoenberg. Later, when I moved to Oxford, I was fortunate in benefiting from the insights of another former student of Schoenberg's, Egon Wellesz. The fact that master and pupil had been on different wavelengths as individuals and composers did not lessen Wellesz's admiration for and fascination with this extraordinary, multi-faceted and complex character. While writing this book, I recalled a number of conversations with Wellesz and belatedly regretted that I had not asked him about this or that, although I am of course aware that responses to factual questions would not have been enough to provide explanations for the many intriguing details of Schoenberg's creative mind.

This volume does not pretend to do much more than refresh aspects of Schoenberg's biography. In a couple of places it has been possible to throw new light on events and issues, and to tidy up uncertainties about dates and personalities. The discussion of Schoenberg's music here is enriched with biographical photographs. I am very grateful for the help I received from Nuria Schoenberg-Nono and Lawrence Schoenberg. Dr Therese Muxeneder and the staff of the Arnold Schönberg Center in Vienna made the writing of this book both easier and more enjoyable and provided invaluable assistance with the illustrations. At the Libraries of the Taylorian Institution and of the Faculty of Music at Oxford I not only found much important material but was also assisted by kind and well-informed staff. Professors Alexander Goehr and Robert Saxton have been sympathetic and indulgent listeners on a number of occasions. Kathryn Bailey Puffett and Christopher Wintle read the entire manuscript and offered perceptive and helpful comments. Professor

Richard Sheppard provided invaluable advice on aspects of German Modernism, and his extensive knowledge of the politics and culture of the Weimar Republic in Germany spared me some embarrassing inaccuracies. In addition, he and my wife Alison have been immensely helpful in filtering out Slavonic and Germanic tendencies from my wayward English.

Finally, a brief note is necessary regarding the two spellings of the composer's surname encountered in this book: Schönberg and Schoenberg. The former is the normal German spelling and was used by him until 1933. In exile, he changed it to Schoenberg and this version is widespread in the English-speaking world, while the Germans tend now to use both spellings, with a preference for the former. In this book the spelling Schoenberg is used throughout to refer to the composer, while for the older members of his family the German spelling is used, even if in places the existence of the two forms side by side appears as an inconsistency.

I

Arnold Schoenberg (left)
with his cousins Edmund,
Rudolf and Malvina
Goldschmied, c. 1885.

On paper it was called the Austro-Hungarian
Monarchy, but in conversation it was called
Austria, a name solemnly abjured officially
while stubbornly retained emotionally, just to
show that feelings are quite as important as
constitutional law and that regulations are one
thing but real life is something else entirely.
Liberal in its constitution, it was administered
clerically. The government was clerical, but
everyday life was liberal. All citizens were
equal before the law, but not everyone was
a citizen.

Robert Musil,
Der Mann ohne Eigenschaften
('The Man Without Qualities')

An Austrian Setting 1874-89

At the time of Arnold Schoenberg's birth in Vienna, in 1874, Austria was very different from the small central European country we know today. The borders of the then Austro-Hungarian Empire stretched from Switzerland in the west to the Ukraine in the east, from southern Poland in the north to the Croatian Adriatic coast in the south. The peoples within these borders belonged to several national and linguistic groups, and were dependent on various social and economic structures. The industrialized heartlands of Bohemia were prosperous, while the rural communities in the Empire's east and in the Balkans were beholden to aristocratic landowners and suffered from chronic poverty and illiteracy. An alternative, nostalgic picture recalls the efficiency of an elaborate system of civil administration and a harmonious coexistence of national groups, irrespective of their differing religious or linguistic affiliations.

By the late 1860s, Hungarian demands for greater autonomy had to be taken seriously in order to help stabilize the Empire that in 1866 had been badly shaken by defeat in a brief war with Prussia. The defeat resulted in the desire of the new Prussian-led Germany to build a culturally and linguistically homogenous state, as opposed to the disparate Austrian one. The *Ausgleich* ('Settlement') with Hungary of 1867 resulted in the new name of Austria-Hungary, the title of *Kaiser und König* ('Emperor and King') for the monarch and a division of the monarchy into its western, Austrian, and eastern, Hungarian parts. As the line of division was near the Leitha, a small river east of Vienna, the western part became known as Cis-Leithania and the eastern one Trans-Leithania. Playing with these names and with the ubiquitous abbreviation of *k. u. k.* (*kaiserlich und königlich*), the novelist Robert Musil called the Dual Monarchy 'Kakania'.

In Cis-Leithania, the Czechs and the Slovenes were beginning to assert their own cultural and linguistic rights, while German speakers were torn between their loyalty to the Habsburg crown, the one secure element that held the diffuse monarchy together, and the idea of a powerful, pan-German community. Non-German speakers, on the other hand, were by no means opposed to Habsburg rule, since they saw in the person of the Emperor a guarantee of some degree of autonomy and a shield against absorption into an assertively German sphere of influence.

It is difficult to divorce such public quandaries from private feelings about identity, culture and religion. In the period following the Settlement of 1867 the question of identity worked its way insidiously into the individual and collective psyches. The resultant insecurity and need for self-examination became moving forces of artistic creativity, and undermined the conservatism that prevailed in Austrian, especially Viennese, artistic circles. As Musil put it, nineteenth-century Austria had 'painted like the Old Masters, written like Goethe and Schiller, and built its houses in the style of the Gothic and the Renaissance'.

Vienna was an ancient capital, boasting an imperial court with an elaborate ritual and an aristocracy that pursued an almost hedonistic, aesthetically pleasing life – one in which the theatricality of the court was carried over into the artistic and cultural life of the city. Painting, for instance, tended to be monumental, and the Court Opera attracted aristocrats and comfortable bourgeois alike. Artistic hedonism was particularly well exemplified by the popularity of that quintessential genre of the Viennese theatre, the operetta. Originally a musical form of political satire, once operetta came to Vienna from Paris it lost its critical edge and became a softer, more exuberant and comedy-led spectacle. Similarly, by the 1860s, the city of Mozart, Beethoven and Schubert had become the city of the waltz composers. But everything in Vienna had two sides, and the frivolous aspects of the city's musical life were reined in by an ambitious bourgeoisie. Within the private sphere, this class regarded music, like literature, as a means of ennobling the human spirit. It was, after all, this domestic musical culture that sustained Brahms, who settled in Vienna in the 1860s, as a composer of piano and chamber music and solo songs. Wagner's music, at least initially, represented the forceful intrusion of an extraneous element. And Wagner felt an animosity towards Vienna precisely because he sensed that its comfortable bourgeois notion of security was easily disturbed by any suggestion of artistic innovation.

Vienna's position as the hub of a large empire meant that its
magnetism extended far. Its development of a modern economy,
albeit a modest one compared with those of London, Paris and
Wilhelmine Berlin, attracted newcomers from all parts of the region.
Nowadays, a quick look at the Vienna telephone book reveals an
astonishing number of Czech, Slovenian and Hungarian surnames
alongside the German ones. Clearly some of these will have had
their origins in post-war upheaval, especially after 1945, but there
have always been many citizens with other than Germanic roots.
Before the Anschluss, Hitler's annexation of Austria in 1938, one
would also have found a large number of Jewish surnames, and
their much diminished presence today is a tragic reminder of a dark
chapter in the recent history of Austria. The multi-ethnic character
of late nineteenth-century Vienna did not remove sources of tension,
and whereas Slav and Hungarian immigrants could be assimilated
by virtue of their Catholicism, the Jews continued to be regarded
as separate. The army and the civil service were essentially Catholic-
dominated, but the educational opportunities provided by the state
enabled Jews to become increasingly prominent in banking, the arts
and medicine. With the large Jewish community being a relatively
recent phenomenon, their prominence became a cause of resentment
on the part of the old Viennese.

Prior to the nineteenth century, the Habsburgs had restricted the
Jewish presence in Vienna. In the early seventeenth century the Jews
were moved from the inner city to what would become the suburb
of Leopoldstadt, outside the city fortifications. Their freedom of
movement was, however, considerably expanded during the reign
of Joseph II in the late eighteenth century, and Leopoldstadt
started to grow. Though sometimes referred to as the ghetto, this
suburb was never a true ghetto (the novelist Joseph Roth called it
'a voluntary ghetto') but rather an area that was favoured by Jews
and other immigrants, especially Czechs.

The golden age for the Viennese Jews came with the accession of
Franz Josef in 1848. As a young monarch he was seen as a modernizer,
a dynamic force who would move Austria forward after the unrest
and the demands for reform that emanated from the revolutionary
year of 1848. The year 1867, when the Emperor granted full citizenship
rights to the Jews, marked the start of a period during which the

Viennese Jewish community would grow and establish a strong presence in the city's cultural and professional élite. By the Anschluss of 1938 there were some 200,000 Jews in Austria, of whom around 180,000 lived in Vienna. The 'Jewish' character of Vienna is therefore a phenomenon of the second half of the nineteenth century, and it coincided with the strengthening of various strands of nationalism, Slav as well as German. In order to gain the loyalty of their adherents, nationalist demagogues resorted only too readily to the demonization of an alleged – Jewish – enemy. Arnold Schoenberg, alongside countless other Austrian Jews, would be, on the one hand,

Emperor Franz Josef and his great-nephew Karl, who succeeded him in 1916 and whose abdication in 1918 marked the end of the Austro-Hungarian Empire.

a beneficiary of the emancipation process, with its expanded cultural and educational opportunities, and, on the other, a victim of the tensions and hatreds that arose from unresolved economic and political problems within a conservative state apparatus.

Arnold's father Samuel settled in Leopoldstadt after a journey that was typical for many young Jews of the time. Samuel Schönberg had been born in 1838 in Szeczeny, a small town near the right bank of the Danube in present-day Hungary. Samuel's family first moved to present-day Bratislava, which at that time was known by its German name of Pressburg and by its Hungarian name of Pozsony. When Samuel moved to Vienna in 1852, he was, according to the arcane rules of citizenship, considered to be domiciled in Pozsony and thus an inhabitant of Trans-Leithania. This anomaly remained an inescapable bureaucratic burden, which then affected his children.

In 1870 Samuel Schönberg married Pauline Nachod, a girl from Prague ten years his junior, whose family had also moved to Vienna. The young family was probably a typical, hard-working Jewish one, fond of reading and of listening to music, while still unable to aspire to any great comfort and security. Samuel had trained in the shoe trade, and in a list of Leopoldstadt tradesmen he was described as a 'manufacturer of footwear goods'. By 1886 he had opened a pawnshop and payments agency in the Kleine Pfarrgasse. In a photograph he appears a somewhat dandyish character, sporting a moustache and longish wavy hair that, according to the Viennese fashion of the time, would have marked him out as a Hungarian. Pauline came from a family of synagogue cantors, and it would seem that the Nachods may have been the source of the musical talent possessed by Samuel and Pauline's children. Pauline's relatives appear to have been quite important in Arnold Schoenberg's early life. An uncle, Fritz Nachod, is believed to have exerted quite a strong formative influence on his nephew, possibly even overshadowing Samuel Schönberg's own role in his son's upbringing. Fritz's son Hans Nachod became a well-established singer – as would Arnold's younger brother Heinrich.

Arnold, born on 13 September 1874, was the Schönbergs' first surviving child; Ottilie followed in 1876 and Heinrich in 1882. At the end of 1881, the Schönberg family unexpectedly grew when Pauline's brother Heinrich and his wife died within a couple of weeks of each other and the orphaned cousins, Melanie and Olga, became for a

Samuel Schönberg, the composer's father. Born in a small Hungarian town, he moved to Vienna in search of a better life.

Opposite, Pauline Schönberg, née Nachod, with her children Ottilie, aged three, and Arnold, aged five, in 1879.

while foster-sisters of the Schönberg children. At the time of Arnold's birth the family lived in Leopoldstadt, at Brigittenau no. 393, which is now Obere Donaustrasse no. 5. Today the street is a wide avenue fronting the Danube Canal, but no. 5 is to be found at its northern end where the road swings inland and becomes narrower. This part still retains the feel of a typical old Viennese residential street, full of tall nineteenth-century apartment buildings.

Leopoldstadt occupies the northern end of an island that is bordered to the east by the main course of the Danube and to the west and south by the Canal that separates the island from the Inner City. The island also contains two large open spaces: the popular Prater lies to the south, while the more formal Augarten park nestles between Leopoldstadt and the borough of Brigittenau further to the north. It was here, in Leopoldstadt, that Arnold was raised and had the formative experiences of his childhood and early youth. By the time Arnold was six-and-a-half, the Schönbergs moved to the Taborstrasse, quite close to the elementary school in the Kleine Pfarrgasse, not far from Samuel's shop. Arnold had become a pupil at that school in April 1880, and the next nine-and-a-half years would be the only period in which he received regular schooling.

After four years in an elementary school, an Austrian boy would have been expected to continue in one of two types of secondary school. The preferred choice for children of ambitious parents from well-to-do families was the élite *Gymnasium* ('grammar school'). Here, an intensive study of classical languages and literature awaited pupils from the age of eleven, although the sciences were by no means neglected. In the *Realschule* ('comprehensive school'), one of which Arnold attended, the stress was on modern languages and the sciences, and pupils were prepared for technical disciplines and practical vocations. In the snobbish atmosphere of Vienna this type of school was regarded as an inferior one, although, in fact, distinguished families often turned to a *Realschule* if they wanted a solid, modern education for their sons. Schoenberg's own artistic sensibilities therefore were nurtured not in an intellectually oriented educational environment but through personal striving on his part to grasp music and literature, and he remained immensely proud of the fact that so much of what he had absorbed as a youth derived from his own tenacity and sense of purpose. Admittedly, the lack of

Opposite, the elegant world of the Ringstrasse in Vienna at the end of the nineteenth century.

a classical education meant that in his musical career he never drew any inspiration from Latin and Greek literature; the Bible remained for him the most powerful depiction of antiquity and the repository of symbolic imagery. And the practical ethos of the *Realschule* never deserted him: he always retained an obsessive urge to create with his hands, to design and improve gadgets, to invent useful tools and objects.

How Schoenberg would have developed beyond the age of fifteen had he remained in regular education can only be a matter for speculation. But at the end of 1889 he experienced the first of the many profound shocks that would influence his life. His father died from influenza, whereupon Arnold was obliged to leave school and become the family breadwinner.

2

An intense young man –
Schoenberg in his late
twenties, c. 1900.

*That the principal contribution to the rise of
the new music should have sprung from the city
of* Der Rosenkavalier *was one of those pranks
of destiny with which it from time to time
establishes a sort of poetic justice.*

Hermann Broch,
Hugo von Hofmannsthal and His Time

Musical Apprenticeship 1889–1901

The death of the breadwinner in a family of such modest income as Schoenberg's meant that the future was looking bleak. His father's death must have been a shock, a shock about which we have very little documentary evidence, but the bereavement would have brought about a profound tension in Schoenberg's character. His years at the *Realschule* had provided him with only the foundations of a broad education. This experience meant that he left the educational process before he could feel alienated by the authoritarian and often unimaginative methods of teaching in Austrian schools. Thus for Schoenberg education remained an unrealized promise, and he would pursue the acquisition of knowledge by whatever means he could. It may be that this denial of educational opportunities instilled in Schoenberg the strong belief that he had a mission to impart his knowledge to others, and to surround himself with people whom he could guide and help to develop. Although much of the teaching that he undertook throughout his life was done as a means of earning money, it is unlikely that he would have persisted at it with such intensity had there not been a deeper motivation, which, like so many other aspects of his character, was established quite early on.

In spring 1891, some eighteen months after he had left school and taken a junior post at the bank of Werner & Co., Schoenberg wrote some passionate letters to his cousin Malvina Goldschmied. Malvina was only fourteen years old, and Arnold not yet seventeen. One might have expected sweet nothings, but instead, in what may be an early attempt to guide and educate someone less experienced than himself, he analysed a letter that Malvina had written to her mother, praising its stylistic and formal properties. Analytical and critical thought was clearly something that came naturally to Schoenberg, and it is not surprising that such high-mindedness was beyond Malvina's understanding. Yet she, too, must have been a sensitive and thinking child. From Arnold's next letter we know that she had expressed the view that the Bible contained nonsense:

You go on to say that you have only disputed the amount of nonsense that is in the Bible; now I must oppose you, as an unbeliever myself, by saying that nowhere in the Bible is there any nonsense. For in it all the most difficult questions concerning morals, law-making, industry and medical science are resolved in the most simple way, often treated from a contemporary point of view.

The 'unbeliever' thus proclaimed the Bible as the foundation of much later thought, while also wondering why his cousin did not believe in a Higher Being. The contradiction here may be no more than an adolescent's expression of his uncertainty as to what path to follow – whether the Judaism that came from his mother's ortho-dox observance, or a free-thinking attitude transmitted to him by his uncle Fritz Nachod, and allegedly shared by his late father.

The novelist Jakob Wassermann has painted the picture of a rather perfunctory religious education being offered in state schools, to various denominations by state-appointed teachers. Termly exam-inations required students to read and comment on religious texts, but there was no insistence on any real or detailed understanding. This attitude may well have suited some of the young Jews at the time, for it enabled them to consider their links to Judaism as vague and unimportant; it was emancipation – a closer integration into the cultural fabric of Austria, and Vienna in particular – which was the order of the day. Schoenberg's youth coincided with that period of Austrian life when Jews increasingly asserted their wish to integrate, and by the turn of the twentieth century Viennese culture was, if not dominated by Jews, then profoundly influenced by them. Their con-tribution to that culture, condemned by the anti-Semites in general and later physically assailed by the Nazis, was by no means sectarian and narrow – on the contrary, it had a depth and universality that transcended the narrow limits of Vienna and largely shaped the image of Vienna as a dynamic city, waking from mid-century conservatism and becoming a potent force in European culture.

But religion was not the only subject covered in this adolescent correspondence. It is from the letters to Malvina Goldschmied that we learn of Schoenberg's early efforts in composition. He had written a new piece, he said, a 'Song without Words', which may be his earliest datable piece. He had started to play the violin at the age of nine, and this instrument remained the basis of his musical experience and the shaping force behind his musical imagination. In an article written at the very end of his life, Schoenberg spoke of his early efforts: 'All my compositions up to about my seventeenth year were no more than imitations of such music as I had been able to become acquainted with – violin duets and duet-arrangements of operas and the repertory of military bands that played in public parks.' Although his mother could play the piano, the family did not own one and Schoenberg never became a confident pianist. String instruments, on the other hand, attracted him and in about 1894 he started to play the cello after a fashion: he bought a large viola in a street market, equipped it with zither strings and pretended that it was a cello, playing it with violin fingering. Only through the intervention of his friends did he manage to acquire a proper cello and learn more about the proper technique of fingering.

Composers who begin by experimenting on the piano are prone to exaggerating the chordal components of music. But by starting as an adventurous string player, Schoenberg would view the progression of melodic lines as a horizontal flow of strands which combine to produce harmonic (vertical) sonorities. Late Romantic thinking emphasized harmonic complexes, masses of superimposed sounds that generated points of density and relaxation. In contrast, counterpoint, the play of lines, had degenerated into a dry academic subject that was taught during professional training but was perceived as belonging to a past age, culminating in the art of Johann Sebastian Bach. Not having been subjected to formal instruction, Schoenberg escaped this prejudice. He also became instinctively aware of linear progression, of the need for each strand of musical texture to make sense as a melodic line instead of being swallowed up in chordal complexes. This is something that the advanced music theory propounded by Heinrich Schenker and Ernst Kurth would begin to address only a decade or so after Schoenberg had already proved the validity of this approach in his works from the turn of the century.

In Schoenberg's Vienna, Johannes Brahms was an example of a composer who did not relegate counterpoint to the status of a pedagogical tool, but made it a living component of his compositional technique. Then again, the progressive faction in the musical world of late nineteenth-century Vienna perceived Brahms as a conservative

A merry band: standing (left to right), Louis Savart, Fritz Kreisler, Eduard Gärtner and Karl Redlich, with the cello-playing Arnold Schoenberg in Redlich's villa at Reichenau bei Payerbach, 8 July 1900.

who still believed in the 'absolute' forms of sonata and symphony, and was disinclined to experiment with bold harmonies. This promoted Wagner as his forward-looking opponent, a visionary who believed in the power of music to depict emotional states and act as a vehicle for symbolic representation. Wagner impressed the younger composers with his rich chromaticism – when chords frequently include notes that do not belong to the prevailing harmony.

The Wagner–Brahms polarization (with Anton Bruckner roped in by the Wagnerians as his Viennese stand-in) informed musical tastes and divided music-lovers into two camps, but Schoenberg, though displaying an allegiance to Brahms, was not an entrenched member of either camp. In the early 1890s he was absorbing music as an autodidact, and in this he differed sharply from the perceived notion of how a composer had to learn his trade. The time when a composer simply amassed his knowledge unsystematically had passed, and

training at a conservatoire was increasingly regarded as the norm.
Both Gustav Mahler and Hugo Wolf, Schoenberg's seniors by
fourteen years, were already submitting themselves to conservatoire
discipline at the age at which Schoenberg wrote his 'Song without
Words'. A closer contemporary, Alexander von Zemlinsky,
Schoenberg's teacher, close friend and later brother-in-law, had
entered the Vienna Conservatoire's preparatory class at the age
of thirteen, advancing to the full course, aged sixteen, while still
following his *Gymnasium* education. Such parallel education was
not uncommon among talented musicians at the time.

In contrast, Schoenberg proceeded in a totally unstructured way.
Music came to him in the open air, at concerts in the Augarten or the
Prater, performed by a military band or one of the popular Viennese
outdoor orchestras that offered a staple diet of operatic overtures and
musical pot-pourri. His friends must have been similarly attracted to
music they could hear for free, and two of them remained in lifelong
contact with Schoenberg, influencing a great deal of his later activity.

David Josef Bach, besides sharing Schoenberg's musical interests,
was one of the friends who introduced him to contemporary poetry
and to the ideals of social democracy, which was then in its infancy
in Austria. Schoenberg later wrote that Bach influenced his character
'by furnishing it with the ethical and moral power needed to with-
stand vulgarity and commonplace popularity'. Schoenberg shared
a similar mixture of interests with Oskar Adler (not a school friend
as is sometimes claimed, since he went to a *Gymnasium* and not a
Realschule). Adler as a young man also espoused left-of-centre Social
Democratic ideals and his developed literary sensibility greatly
influenced Schoenberg's own literary enthusiasms. He introduced
Schoenberg to music theory and provided him with an opportunity
to play in his string quartet.

Bach eventually became a music critic and led the Social Democratic Party's cultural department, giving him responsibility for
workers' concerts. Adler pursued a bafflingly varied career as a
medical doctor, the leader of a string quartet and an authority on
astrology. During and after World War II, as a refugee in London,
he continued with his astrological interests while as a performer he
exercised a profound influence on a young Viennese fellow-émigré,
Hans Keller, who would become a leading music critic in England.

Schoenberg's earliest encounters with orchestral music came through open-air concerts by military bands in Viennese parks, such as this one.

In 1894 Schoenberg joined Polyhimnia, a Leopoldstadt-based amateur music society, and was for a while the only cellist in its orchestra. Adler, too, played in the orchestra and it was very likely he who had introduced Schoenberg to Alexander von Zemlinsky, then the orchestra's conductor. Although, like Schoenberg, Zemlinsky was from Leopoldstadt, the cultural roots and early childhoods of the two men differed considerably. Zemlinsky was the son of a Catholic who had converted to Judaism in order to marry his Jewish bride, Clara Semo. The Semo family had come to Vienna in the 1860s from Bosnia, then a Turkish province. Unlike the majority of the Viennese Jews, who belonged to the Ashkenazy tradition, the Semos were Sephardic, descendants of those Jews who had settled in the Balkans after expulsion from Spain in the late fifteenth century. Zemlinsky accordingly went to a Sephardic elementary school, and the family attended a Sephardic synagogue. The cultural mix of Leopoldstadt thus meant that Zemlinsky had to integrate on two levels. He needed to join the culturally dominant Ashkenazy community, which tended to look down on the 'provincial' Sephardis; and he had to overcome Viennese petty anti-Semitism in order to progress in the musical world by the force of his own talent and commitment. It is therefore not surprising that he and Schoenberg felt an emotional bond that must also have provided a firm basis for their quasi teacher–pupil relationship.

Zemlinsky was only three years Schoenberg's senior, but as he had been through the rigorous conservatoire training and was an able composer, he was in a position to impart some shape to Schoenberg's fairly unsystematic musical knowledge. Apart from Josef Labor, a blind organist who offered Schoenberg some encouragement but no instruction, Zemlinsky was the only teacher Schoenberg ever had. The speed with which the twenty-year-old bank clerk imbibed knowledge and the breadth of the musical repertory with which he became familiar through the analysis of scores were evidently phenomenal – probably telling us more about Schoenberg's quick mind than Zemlinsky's guidance. Schoenberg thought of himself as a Brahmsian until he met Zemlinsky, whose orientation was broader and encompassed Wagner too. It is interesting that Schoenberg – in his later years and in spite of his laudatory comments about Wagner and the recognizable Wagnerian traits in his early music – did not regard Wagner as a model from whom he learned; he retained an underlying loyalty to Brahms.

Schoenberg's horizon would soon extend to include Richard Strauss. Strauss was, after all, considered to be the most progressive composer of the time in the German cultural orbit, while Mahler's reputation was that of a composer who stood in Strauss's shadow. Although Strauss was four years younger, he came to prominence earlier than Mahler did, and captivated the audience with his brilliantly orchestrated tone poems. The sheer length of Mahler's symphonies and his combinations of the lyrical and sarcastic, of march music and the ländler, taxed the audience's power of comprehension; time would be needed for his greatness to be recognized. As a young man, Schoenberg, too, needed some time to begin to appreciate Mahler; later he said that once he understood Mahler, he rejected Strauss.

Opposite, 'Alex' – Alexander von Zemlinsky, Schoenberg's near-contemporary, his good friend, brother-in-law and for a short time in the 1890s his only teacher of composition.

Soon after joining Polyhimnia, Schoenberg won the society's composition prize with the song *Schilflied*, and again in October 1894 with three piano pieces which bore the unmistakeable traces of the idiom of Brahms and Antonín Dvořák. Schoenberg by this time was determined to be a musician, and so he rejoiced at the loss of his job following the bankruptcy of his employer in 1895. According to David Josef Bach, Schoenberg burst into his home and ecstatically announced that his career as a clerk was over – from now on he was to be a musician. In his new profession the first meagre income that he earned derived from conducting workers' choirs, an activity probably arranged for him by Bach and Adler.

It is difficult to gauge the depth of Schoenberg's commitment to the workers' cause. He seems to have gone along with some Social Democratic sentiments, while primarily welcoming the opportunity for advancing his musical skills and picking up a modest income. He started by conducting the Meidling male voice choir and the choir of the metalworkers' association in the suburb of Stockerau. But the engagement that made a stronger impact on him was his work with the male-voice choir 'Freisinn' in Mödling, a town some ten miles south of Vienna. Schoenberg recalled that the members of the choir took him to be one of them and addressed him as 'comrade', but that it was not long before the bourgeois in him turned out to be stronger.

The seemingly conflicting requirements of a choice between social engagement and devotion to one's own creative activity were at that time felt very strongly by an entire generation of Austrian and German artists. This generation found itself caught up in the pulsating activity of a Vienna energized by a host of personalities in the arts, literature and politics who, in the last two decades of the nineteenth century, were shaking up that conservative and artistically cautious city. Scandinavian literature was embraced by the young literati, for Henrik Ibsen had opened up the possibility of seeing literature as a mode of social criticism. Politics and culture became intertwined in a way unknown in Vienna in earlier decades, and numerous literary reputations were formed or lost through this mixture of art and politics. By the mid 1890s the writer and critic Hermann Bahr had emerged to inspire and galvanize literary and artistic activity. He had spent time in Paris and Berlin, and on returning to Vienna in 1891 introduced the Viennese to French Symbolist literature and new

German poetry. In his younger days Bahr had made some unsavoury
anti-Semitic statements, but now he renounced politics and advocated
art as the expression of morality. He also proclaimed nervous energy
as the motivating force behind artistic creativity. Karl Kraus, the
acerbic Viennese critic, saw this as a dangerous manifestation of *l'art
pour l'art*, and, in typically Viennese fashion, a bitter and ultimately
lengthy dispute arose between the two men.

Even if not directly inspired by Bahr, Schoenberg's belief in creative activity as the embodiment of a deep personal conviction had
much in common with Bahr's ideas. But just as he was able to admire
Brahms as well as Wagner and Strauss, Schoenberg was also drawn
to Kraus, particularly in the early years of the twentieth century.
A loner, not unlike Schoenberg, and similarly endowed with a prodigious memory, Kraus was a poet, satirist, actor, critic and editor of
the periodical *Die Fackel* ('The Torch'), which he largely wrote himself.
He was driven by a mission to expose the misuse and debasement of
language – both in the inflated style of late nineteenth-century prose
and in careless, yet manipulative, use of language in politics.

Most accounts of Viennese Modernism stress that the decade between about 1895 and 1905 was dominated in the visual arts by the
new aesthetics of the Secession, itself an adaptation of the ideals of
the English Pre-Raphaelites and French art nouveau. The Secessionists rebelled against the prevailing academicism in Austrian late
nineteenth-century art and sought to replace stale figurative painting
with striking representations of the human body and bold use of
colour. Indeed, for a while the term 'Secessionist' was used in Vienna
to describe artistic innovation in general. The Secession's innovations
in painting, architecture and design were so influential largely because
Austrian nineteenth-century culture tended to place the visual arts
above literature. It is, however, difficult to establish a causal link
between music and the visual art of the Secession, and attempts to
equate the complex contrapuntal lines of Schoenberg's early music and
the finely wrought details of Gustav Klimt's and Koloman Moser's
painting appear forced and superficial. The point of departure for the
musicians seems more likely to have been the works of such highly
original writers as Hugo von Hofmannsthal, Richard Beer-Hofmann,
Arthur Schnitzler and Bahr, and, even more, the psychologically
inspired dramas of August Strindberg and the new poetic voices from

Germany – Richard Dehmel and Stefan George. Schoenberg's
tendency to take new poetic texts as starting points, even for instrumental compositions, reveals his own rootedness in literature. This
is particularly true of his string sextet *Verklärte Nacht* (1899), to
which we shall return later. This chamber music piece would clearly
endorse Bahr's belief expressed in his 1891 essay '*Die Überwindung des
Naturalismus*' ('The Overcoming of Naturalism') that 'once the
nervous energy has been fully released, and the human being, particularly the artist, has become entirely surrendered to his nerves
without any thought of rational and sense-derived reflexion, then art
will recover its lost freedom'.

Schoenberg spent the three years after he met Zemlinsky searching
for an individual voice, and the surviving evidence of his compositional activity shows him investigating various possibilities. Richard
Heuberger encouraged him to explore the piano idiom. His membership of Polyhimnia led him to compose the pieces for string orchestra
that he started in spring 1897, while his participation in Adler's
quartet resulted in a string quartet that he showed to Zemlinsky in
the same year. Zemlinsky suggested some revisions and, as he was
on the committee of the influential Viennese Tonkünstlerverein
(Composers' Society), he recommended his friend's quartet for one
of the society's private concerts. The quartet, bearing the stamp of
Brahms and Dvořák as befitted a self-confessed Brahmsian, met with
a warm reception at its first performance and was included in the
Tonkünstlerverein's series of public concerts in the following year.
According to an unsubstantiated anecdote told by Schoenberg's
cousin Hans Nachod, the influential music critic Eduard Hanslick
commented: 'Are we witnessing a new Mozart here?' If true, this
ought not to be taken as Hanslick's opinion on the style of the music.
He was more likely observing that Schoenberg – despite a lack of
musical training – was capable of creating a work that seemed to have
descended into his consciousness miraculously and fully formed.

In the Viennese context, composing in a Brahmsian idiom was
a guarantee of acceptance, something that Schoenberg did not seek
as an end in itself. Rather, composition was for him a process of
learning, from himself as much as from others, and the works that he
produced during 1898 also included songs that look towards Hugo
Wolf and Strauss. Schoenberg's search and self-examination did not,

however, stop at music. He was not easily led by others, and therefore the momentous decision, which he took in March 1898, to leave the Jewish faith and become a Protestant must have been more than a response to the influence of his Protestant friend Walter Pieau, who is credited with inspiring this action. Conversion to Christianity was not uncommon among Austrian Jews at the time. Although sometimes a pragmatic, even opportunistic, move by those who wanted promotion in the civil service, conversion was often a religious affirmation of the desire to embrace fully the German culture and bourgeois values to which Austrian Jews aspired. 'Through emancipation to salvation' was the maxim adopted by Kraus, who also left the Jewish community in that year. Mahler's conversion to Catholicism in 1897 was by no means insincere, yet it was also an act of prudence at the time when, as Director of the Court Opera, he was employed by one of the central institutions of the Catholic Habsburg establishment. In Schoenberg's case there was no opportunistic career motivation and the action arose out of personal conviction, much to the consternation of his Jewish family. Yet his conversion to Protestantism came at the wrong moment.

Under pressure from various national movements, the old Austrian liberalism all but collapsed in the last years of the nineteenth century. Within Austria itself, the idea of a multinational Austria-Hungary was being opposed more and more vigorously by a vociferous and xenophobic pan-German movement. By 1895 Vienna found itself with an anti-Semitic lord mayor in the person of the charismatic demagogue Karl Lueger. In 1898 the right-wing politician Georg von Schönerer launched his 'Los von Rom' ('Away from Rome') movement, which rested on three principles: opposition to the house of Habsburg; distrust of Catholicism in favour of Protestantism as an 'authentic' German religious manifestation; and, of course, the obligatory anti-Semitism. Schoenberg may have been motivated by a genuine desire to replace his Judaism with a broader and more 'modern' religious faith, and the importance accorded by Protestants to the Old Testament made his choice more logical than a move to Catholicism. Nevertheless, he joined the Protestant community at the precise time when it was being wooed by the likes of Schönerer. Schoenberg may have experienced his departure from the Jewish community as a form of liberation, as did many other young Viennese Jews who wished to

demonstrate decisively that they considered themselves equal participants in the shaping of liberal German culture. Unfortunately,
those whom he joined included too many anti-Semites for Schoenberg
ever to feel at home in his new-found Christianity. Many years later,
writing to his pupil Peter Gradenwitz, he admitted that he had
never been comfortable with Protestantism. Publicly he continued
to be perceived as a Jew, and during the rest of his time in Europe
he would experience unpleasant outbursts of anti-Semitism.

If the string quartet was still the work of a follower of earlier masters,
Schoenberg's next chamber music work signalled an enormous change.
The string sextet *Verklärte Nacht*, which Schoenberg finished in late
1899, was, for the staid Viennese critics at least, a challenge to tradition
and subversive on several levels. It was based on a poem by the German
Naturalist poet Richard Dehmel, who had the reputation of being on
the political Left and was the author of unashamedly erotic poetry.
Even if the imagery of Dehmel's *Verklärte Nacht* was restrained
in comparison with his more outspoken works, it was perceived in
Vienna as unsettling, while Schoenberg's score appeared to subvert
the hallowed autonomy of chamber music by casting the work as a
one-movement narrative in the manner of a symphonic poem. This
now enormously popular work has often been subjected to analyses
that seek to relate parts of the score to those parts of the poem
which consist of short exchanges between a man and a woman,
punctuated by reflections in the poet's voice. The woman confesses
that she is carrying someone else's child, but the man responds
that the strength of his love encompasses both the woman and the
child. The man's response is, moreover, presented in a Wagner-like
context, where the feelings of floating, of warmth and of the union of
bodies, are suggested with strong sexual overtones. In fact, the poem
provided Schoenberg with only a framework, a way of controlling a
long and complex musical substance, and the work's true inspiration
may well have been an actual love affair. Schoenberg spent the
summer and early autumn of 1899 in Payerbach near Vienna, in the
company of Zemlinsky and his sister Mathilde. The sextet was
largely written between September and December that year, and its
passionate, even orgiastic, moments speak of an intense personal
experience, the beginning of Schoenberg's relationship with Mathilde
which would lead to the couple's marriage.

Before writing the sextet, in the summer of 1899 Schoenberg completed four solo songs, three with texts by Dehmel, which are among the earliest of his works to bear opus numbers. The rich chromaticism, recalling Wagner and Strauss, and the resulting expressive tension are carried much further in the sextet and testify both to an awakening of personal passion and to an enormous advance in Schoenberg's mastery of a complex harmonic texture which emerges as the result of an interplay of contrapuntal lines. The sextet's opening may owe something to that of Strauss's Symphony in F minor. Indeed, the reference may have been a deliberate one, as if to signify an allegiance not just to Strauss but to a particular expressive ideal, for it mixes echoes of Strauss with camouflaged references to Wagner's *Tristan und Isolde*. Yet the sextet's rich sonorities, even if reminiscent of Strauss, and its complex harmonic texture were achieved through an interplay of independent contrapuntal lines – which ultimately derives from Brahms's string sextets. Schoenberg's ability both to understand the structural principles behind the music he had encountered in his formative years and to re-interpret them in a remarkably

The German Naturalist poet Richard Dehmel, author of the poem *Verklärte Nacht* that inspired Schoenberg's string sextet of the same name.

original manner was fully demonstrated in this early masterpiece. When the work was eventually performed in public, in March 1902, Schoenberg was living in Berlin, and he did not witness the hostile reaction of the notoriously conservative Viennese public and critics; the performance marked the beginning of his troubled relationship with the Viennese musical establishment.

Schoenberg's assimilation of influences that led to *Verklärte Nacht* was not achieved through systematic training. He learned by copying, by assisting Zemlinsky in the preparation of piano reductions, and by undertaking the orchestration of operettas for various Viennese composers whose gift for churning out attractive tunes far surpassed their ability to give final polished form to their inventions. The project to which Schoenberg turned immediately after *Verklärte Nacht* – the monumental oratorio *Gurrelieder* – saw him combining his early experience of writing solo songs with his ability to control larger dramatic structures, something he had absorbed while working alongside Zemlinsky. At around the time of a competition held by the Tonkünstlerverein for a song cycle (a competition to which Zemlinsky may have alerted his friend), Schoenberg wrote several solo songs with texts from the narrative poem *Gurresange* by the Danish poet Jens Peter Jacobsen, but neither Schoenberg nor Zemlinsky felt that the songs would stand much chance in the competition. Nevertheless, Schoenberg's interest in Jacobsen was now greatly aroused.

As already mentioned, Scandinavian writers were widely read in intellectual circles in Germany and Austria in the late nineteenth century. Ibsen was soon eclipsed by the more modern and psychologically orientated August Strindberg, who was to remain an important influence on the Viennese musical avant garde. Zemlinsky's opera *Es war einmal* (1897–9) was based on a play by the Danish novelist and poet Holger Drachmann, and Schoenberg naturally followed his friend in the exploration of new Scandinavian poetry. Jacobsen's complete works appeared in German in 1899, and the presence in Vienna of the Danish composer Ludwig Schytte, who in 1896 published his song cycle *Tove*, consisting of seven of the *Gurresange* poems, could well have acted as an additional stimulus. Schytte, like other Danish composers, was drawn to the lyrical aspects of the story of the lovers Waldemar ('Valdemar' in Jacobsen's

Opposite, Dank, Op. 1, No. 1 in Schoenberg's hand (1898). The score, printed in 1903, was dedicated: 'To my friend and teacher Alexander von Zemlinsky'.

spelling) and Tove, and avoided the problematic portions of the poem dealing with King Waldemar's rebellion against God and his subsequent damnation. Schoenberg, who must have been attracted to the psychologically intense culmination of the narrative, could have felt that a conventional song-cycle genre would be inappropriate and that a more ambitious and extended dramatic treatment of the story was called for.

In the context of Jacobsen's tale of the ill-fated love between Waldemar and the young Tove, who is killed by the jealous Queen, both Wagner and Dehmel come to mind. But, instead of a Wagnerian insistence on dramatic seamlessness, Schoenberg conceived the lyrical exchanges between the lovers as a gigantic song cycle. In its piano reduction the first part of the complex orchestral score is still playable on the piano, betraying the work's origin in the idea of a song cycle. But the rest – the narrative of Tove's death that is presented by the voice of the wood dove, and the concluding wild chase of Waldemar and his men, who are made to suffer eternal damnation as punishment for Waldemar's daring denunciation of God as a tyrant – becomes in Schoenberg's hands something else. It is in fact the extraordinary fusion of a symphonic poem, the culmination of an act from a music drama, and a late Romantic restructuring of a spatial expanse reminiscent of Hector Berlioz. Only a strong-willed and self-assured composer could have dared to undertake such a task. When the work was eventually completed in 1911, it was shown to be a masterful blend of Wagner's and Strauss's orchestral writing and of Brahms's vocal idiom. The influence of Zemlinsky's large-scale cantata *Frühlingsbegräbnis* ('The Burial of Spring', 1896) is also detectable.

The first part of the task, the composition of the basic musical texture, was accomplished with speed and single-minded dedication, traits that would emerge over the next two decades as key to Schoenberg's personality. He later told Alban Berg that he composed most of the work during March and April of 1900, leaving only the third part incomplete. Operetta orchestrations, a necessary source of income, intervened at that point, and the third part of the *Gurrelieder* was eventually completed in early 1901. Although this time frame is essentially correct, the sketches betray many revisions and reworkings, as is to be expected with a work of such large dimensions. Indeed,

the orchestration proved to be a task that would stretch over a whole
decade, during which time Schoenberg's musical language moved
so far from the late Romantic, post-Wagnerian idiom in which the
Gurrelieder had been originally conceived that it required an enormous
investment of will to return to it. Of course, it was not the same
Schoenberg who in 1911 tackled the *Gurrelieder* again. Whatever
orchestral sound he had had in mind around 1900 was not going

A posed portrait of Gertrude
(Trudi) and Mathilde
Schönberg taken c. 1907.

to re-emerge years later in an uncontaminated guise. Rather, it had benefited from his gradual mastery of orchestration that evolved through such works as *Pelleas und Melisande*, Five Orchestral Pieces and even *Erwartung*, which closely preceded the completion of the *Gurrelieder*.

The time and concentration needed for completing the *Gurrelieder* were hard to find in what was an eventful period of Schoenberg's life. When he and Mathilde Zemlinsky married, in October 1901, Mathilde was already expecting their first child, Gertrude, who was born in 1902, and Schoenberg, in addition to having to help his widowed mother, needed now to support his new family. As luck would have it (and a curious piece of luck it must have been), a Berlin cabaret directed by Ernst von Wolzogen was on tour in the summer and autumn of 1901. A quarrel had recently erupted between Wolzogen and his resident composer, Oscar Straus. Straus wanted to extricate himself from Wolzogen's troupe and a fortuitous meeting between Wolzogen and Schoenberg resulted in Schoenberg's first salaried job since his days as a bank clerk. He was offered the position of music director in the new Berlin premises of the Buntes Theater, where Wolzogen's cabaret was due to open in November 1901.

3

Schoenberg at the turn of
the twentieth century.

*I had the feeling as if I had fallen into an ocean
of boiling water, and not knowing how to swim
or to get out in another manner, I tried with
my legs and arms as best as I could.*

*I do not know what saved me; why I was
not drowned or cooked alive. I have perhaps
only one merit: I never gave up!*

Arnold Schoenberg,
June 1947

An Ocean of Boiling Water 1901-8

There were obvious similarities as well as profound differences between turn-of-the-century Vienna and Berlin. Both cities were the
capitals of German-speaking empires – Vienna at the heart of a well-
established conglomerate of nations, an Empire beset by internal
crises, and Berlin the confident and expanding capital of the recently
unified Germany. In both cities tensions existed between conservative imperial courts and liberal bourgeois institutions, between
entrenched aristocratic circles and reformist associations, although
there seemed to be more interest in innovative art in Berlin.
Schoenberg had already experienced some of the tensions between
the old and the new in Vienna, and this made him uncomfortable
and impatient to break through institutional barriers. His interest
in the work of modern German poets (whom he preferred to his
Austrian contemporaries) had already directed his thoughts towards
Berlin, and Wolzogen's offer appeared unusually attractive.

Ernst von Wolzogen was himself a newcomer to Berlin. Previously
active in Munich, he had written a witty libretto for Richard Strauss's
opera *Feuersnot*. When he moved to Berlin in 1900, the city had

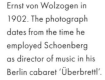

Ernst von Wolzogen in
1902. The photograph
dates from the time he
employed Schoenberg
as director of music in his
Berlin cabaret 'Überbrettl'.

several theatres offering light entertainment. It is said that fatigue caused by work left Berliners with little appetite or energy for serious art and that the 'Tingeltangel' theatres, as they became known, provided much-needed relief. In addition, German Modernism in general showed a penchant for popular art as an antidote to the heaviness of late Romanticism. The poet Otto Julius Bierbaum pioneered a type of 'applied poetry' which looked towards the popular ballad. His anthology *Deutsche Chansons* (1900), in which he included work by Schoenberg's favourite poet Dehmel, came to the composer's notice, and it seems that almost immediately he set to music several of its poems (by Bierbaum, Frank Wedekind and Gustav Falke).

When Schoenberg showed these songs to Wolzogen in the summer of 1901, Wolzogen realized that this was the man he was looking for: someone highly motivated artistically, and also able to enhance the prestige of the superior kind of cabaret that he was determined to establish in Berlin. Wolzogen no doubt also hoped that Schoenberg would continue to experience the enormous success that Oscar Straus had enjoyed as his resident composer – but this was not to be. Schoenberg's position was not easy: Straus was an able improviser and accompanist, while Schoenberg was a poor pianist. He had to concentrate on orchestrating other people's work, and even though his *Nachtwandlerlied*, one of the settings that he had brought with him from Vienna, was written in a witty and jaunty cabaret style, it did not find favour with the Berlin public. In only a matter of weeks, in January 1902, Wolzogen had managed to lure Straus back and he, of course, eclipsed Schoenberg. In May, Wolzogen, who had overreached himself financially, had to give up the directorship of the Buntes Theater. Schoenberg's six-month contract was in any case about to expire and his only steady source of income was again provided by hack work – orchestrating operetta scores and preparing piano reductions for the Viennese publisher, Universal Edition.

When Schoenberg left Vienna for Berlin, the Court Opera was under the imaginative directorship of Gustav Mahler. Yet Schoenberg had little understanding of Mahler's music at that time: his closeness to and eventual adoration of Mahler would come a few years later. There is, rather, a trace of Richard Strauss in Schoenberg's early songs as well as in *Verklärte Nacht*, and now he found himself in Berlin and near the composer whose reputation was on the increase

The stage of the Berlin
Buntes Theater, designed
by August Endell, where
Wolzogen's 'Überbrettl'
opened in January 1901.

throughout the German-speaking world. Strauss and Schoenberg first
met in spring 1902; Strauss was immediately impressed by the younger
man, and saw in him not just a composer of immense promise but
also a useful and, initially, willing amanuensis. Among the works
that Strauss entrusted to Schoenberg for copying was his setting of
the nineteenth-century poet Ludwig Uhland's *Taillefer*, conceived
for three soloists, an eight-part choir and a large symphony orchestra.
As Schoenberg had returned to the orchestration of the *Gurrelieder*
by June 1902, his acquaintance with Strauss's elaborate score can only
have encouraged him to persist with his intention of deploying similarly large forces. In October 1902 *Verklärte Nacht* was performed in
Berlin and this must have further disposed Strauss in his favour, as
he not only helped Schoenberg to obtain a teaching post at the Stern
Conservatoire but was also responsible for Schoenberg's successful
application for a grant from the Liszt Foundation.

Schoenberg's first sketches for the symphonic poem *Pelleas und
Melisande*, based on Maurice Maeterlinck's Symbolist play of 1892, date
from his initial contacts with Strauss. It is not clear whether Strauss
alerted him to the play; nevertheless, Strauss's presence is again felt
in the score, even though Schoenberg was so eager to achieve a full and
varied orchestral sound that the orchestral texture often appears over-
saturated. 'The instrumentation appears to me not quite faultless,'

Zemlinsky wrote to Schoenberg when he first saw the full score. Yet Schoenberg did not revise it after this. Indeed, this plenitude emerges as an essential part of the work's identity. The complexity of the score, its richness of expression surpassing anything Strauss had written, and the intricacy of the one-movement form (which cradles within itself elements of a full sonata cycle) demanded of the listener a great deal of concentration. And this abundance of activity often seemed relentless, without the moments of relaxation customarily provided by Strauss in his symphonic poems. Towards the end of his life Schoenberg said that he had originally intended to write an opera on the subject and was unaware of Claude Debussy's opera,

The first page of the autograph score of *Pelleas und Melisande*, dated Berlin, 28 February 1903.

then in progress. It was only his belief that he would achieve a better characterization through the symphonic medium that decided him against an operatic form.

By early spring 1903 Schoenberg's financial position in Berlin had become so precarious that a return to Vienna, where he could rely on some help from his friends, was the only reasonable way out. This meant that he was no longer able to foster links with Berlin musicians in order to secure a performance of *Pelleas* there. His stay in Berlin was a failure if it is viewed as an attempt to ensure some financial security for himself and his family; when they left Berlin they were as poor as they had been before Schoenberg accepted Wolzogen's contract. Nevertheless Berlin had in some senses been a less restrictive environment than Vienna (there was greater tolerance for artists who were trying to break established moulds), and his coming to the attention of Strauss, and influential composer Ferruccio Busoni too, had given him new openings that he had previously lacked. He also signed his first publishing contract with the Dreililien-Verlag, a firm directed by the composer Max Marschalk, who was to remain Schoenberg's supporter for some time to come. In Berlin Schoenberg had not been affected by hostile opinions emanating from established cliques, a constant feature of Viennese musical life, and the relatively speedy completion of *Pelleas* coloured his impression of Berlin as a place where he could devote himself to serious work. Later, as he wished to escape the oppressive atmosphere of Vienna, he became attracted to Berlin again.

Schoenberg was not alone in experiencing life in Vienna as a continuing paradox. The café culture of the city provided a forum for lively critical debates and exchanges of ideas. But the very intensity of the exchanges and the habit-forming circles established in the various cafés also meant that disputes often flared up, and close friendships suffered setbacks, only for the opponents to be reconciled later on. As a musician with a lively interest in literature and painting Schoenberg was, of course, drawn to these arguments but not necessarily bound to any of the groups. He therefore managed to remain connected to individuals who were barely on speaking terms with each other. For example, throughout the long-lasting breach between Kraus and Bahr, Schoenberg maintained friendly links with them both.

Stefan George,
authoritarian leader of a
circle of German poets.
His rarefied poetry attracted
Schoenberg in his search
for pure expression.

Close discipleships were not typical of Vienna in the early phase of the modern movement, although they were a phenomenon associated with German poets and artists. In Germany, Stefan George was a particularly charismatic personality who assembled around him a group of younger poets – but when he tried to draw Hofmannsthal into his circle, Hofmannsthal resisted, preferring his Viennese detachment. The atmosphere in Vienna, however, was changing fast between about 1901 and 1903. The Secessionists, who had come into their own as a group in 1898, were forced to form an association since this appeared to be the only effective way of countering official disapproval of new forms of art. Nevertheless, by around 1905 they were already perceived by those close to Kraus as followers of an ideology too close to late Romantic art. In addition to their emotionally charged images, the Secessionists had retained their trust in formal control, while Schoenberg found himself much more in sympathy with the emerging aesthetics that valued expression and raw nervous energy above all else and eventually gave the name to Expressionism.

Zemlinsky had resigned from the Tonkünstlerverein by 1903, because he had become aware of the gap that was opening between an institution rooted in the older, Brahmsian ideology and the new inquiring spirit of younger artists. Mahler, too, was isolated as a composer, despite his influential position at the Opera, and the growing closeness between him and the younger Zemlinsky and Schoenberg derived from his need for understanding and support. Mahler's personal relationship with Zemlinsky could not have been easy, however. Some years earlier Zemlinsky had fallen in love with his composition pupil Alma Schindler, and her diaries reveal a disturbing mix of adolescent, Wagner-tinted outpourings of love and complaints about her teacher's physical appearance. It was not long after their passionate affair came to an inevitable end that Alma met and married Gustav Mahler, though she remained on friendly terms with Zemlinsky. Alma did not at first find Schoenberg agreeable company – the solidly bourgeois girl was upset by his bohemian appearance and attitudes. But, like many others, then and later, she soon became fascinated by his personality.

Despite a fiercely asserted independence in matters intellectual and artistic, at this time Schoenberg needed to have close to him

The height of bourgeois elegance: Alma Schindler-Mahler. Herself a promising composer and pupil of Zemlinsky, she gave up composition at her husband's request.

someone on whom he could rely for encouragement, as if looking for a father-substitute. Strauss may have appeared at one time to be this source of support, but he was too absorbed in promoting his own career to show any real sympathy towards the younger man. Mahler seemed more disposed to assume such a role; many of his remarks about Schoenberg show him to be a concerned protector who may at times have felt that he was dealing with a rebellious teenager. Schoenberg easily provoked quarrels, but equally believed that a deeper understanding of shared artistic beliefs would overcome any temporary disagreements. Despite Schoenberg's outburst of temper towards him, and a temporary cooling of relations in around 1905, Mahler retained his faith in a composer whose extraordinary talent and creative force he could recognize even though he was unable to identify with his music. Mahler, who still believed in the broad narrative structures of the symphony, was taxed by Schoenberg's tendency to use dense musical textures; the resulting scores troubled Mahler since he could not easily play them on the piano. Alma recalls that Mahler commented in 1906: 'If I often do not understand him, this is because I am old and he is young – hence, he is right.' That Mahler felt 'old' in comparison with Schoenberg sounds like

Mahler and Strauss in Graz for the performance of *Salome*, 16 May 1906. The 'scandalous' opera was forbidden in Vienna by the Court censor, so Mahler, and a party which also included Schoenberg, Egon Wellesz and Alban Berg, travelled to Graz to see it.

a poetic exaggeration, but it had a grain of truth. Shifts in aesthetic preferences and the understanding of artistic aims were rapid and momentous in Vienna, and Mahler belonged to the *fin-de-siècle* movement, not far in its aesthetics from the Secessionists. Moreover, Mahler was welcome in the salons of the enlightened Jewish *haute bourgeoisie*, such as the one presided over by Bertha Zuckerkandl, the daughter of the proprietor of the *Neue Wiener Tagblatt*. In contrast, Schoenberg was part of a group of self-consciously progressive artists who were looking for a new direction, and who were more attuned to new poetry and drama.

The first attempt to set up a musical society in Vienna with the aim of promoting contemporary music was made by a young lawyer, Wilhelm von Wymetal, and a university student called Paul Stefan. They met Schoenberg during his final months in Berlin and on his return to Vienna they drew him into their circle. Their Ansorge Society had chosen to promote the music of the German composer and pianist Conrad Ansorge, hardly a force to be reckoned with as far as Schoenberg was concerned. From this, nevertheless, there emerged a forum that for some years from November 1903 presented to the Viennese a mixture of literary and musical events, in which

Dr Eugenie Schwarzwald, known to her acquaintances as 'Frau Doktor', a progressive reformer of education and a patron of young artists, including Oskar Kokoschka, Schoenberg, Adolf Loos and Robert Musil.

both Zemlinsky and Schoenberg were represented as composers. Possibly encouraged by the example of the Ansorge Society, Zemlinsky, Franz Schmidt, Schoenberg and several others launched the Vereinigung schaffender Tonkünstler (Society of Creative Musicians) in 1904. This drew enthusiastic support from Mahler and his friend Guido Adler, the influential head of the Institute of Musicology at Vienna University.

In around 1904 another Viennese circle formed around the educational reformer Eugenie Schwarzwald. This was more of a forum for those whom Mahler would have regarded as 'young', since the group challenged the Secessionists' aesthetics while developing its own ideas in response to the new critical thought that was emerging in the early years of the century. Schoenberg was introduced to the Schwarzwald circle by his friend, the architect Adolf Loos, and some years later the group included Loos's protégé, Oskar Kokoschka, and the novelist Robert Musil. Musil came into contact with this circle in 1909 and left a somewhat tongue-in-cheek description of its flavour and dynamics in his novel *Der Mann ohne Eigenschaften* ('The Man without Qualities'). Here Eugenie Schwarzwald becomes Ermelinda Tutzi, nicknamed Diotima (after the classical-Romantic poet Friedrich Hölderlin's ideal woman), and her gatherings, Musil says:

> … *were celebrated for the fact that on her 'great days' one ran into people one could not exchange a single word with because they were too well known in some special field or other for small talk … In general, things were so arranged that a random mixture blended harmoniously, except for the young intellectuals, whom Diotima usually kept apart by means of special invitations, and those rare or special guests whom she had a way of unobtrusively singling out and providing with a special setting.*

Frau Doktor, as Eugenie Schwarzwald was generally known, was a woman of action, the founder of a progressive school for girls, and she was determined to shake up the traditional Austrian education system. She had become aware of Schoenberg's prodigious talent, and on finding that he relied for his living on occasional teaching and some editorial work, invited him to hold classes when her school building was not otherwise needed. During the academic year 1904–5, therefore, a small, informal conservatoire came into being, with Zemlinsky and Schoenberg teaching harmony and composition and Elsa Bienenfeld teaching the history of music. The classes soon became too demanding and only the more dedicated participants persisted, essentially those students of musicology at Vienna University who came to Schoenberg at the recommendation of Guido Adler. None of them could have been prepared for what they found. Exposed hitherto to a conservative, rule-laden method of teaching composition, the students encountered in Schoenberg a mind of exceptional intensity, a teacher who seemed capable, both as an artist and as a theorist, of grasping a rich repertoire of the classics of the Austro-German tradition from Bach to Wagner. These he analysed with a phenomenal quickness of mind and an ability to draw far-reaching inferences.

The students, having very different personalities, reacted to Schoenberg – then and in the years that followed – in very different ways. Anton von Webern, born in 1883, had been composing for a while and was contemplating a further course of studies with Hans Pfitzner. However, Schoenberg's analytical approach to composition, coupled with Webern's own scholarly work on the music of the late fifteenth century, enabled the younger man to develop an original style characterized by brevity, structural clarity and austerity of expressive means. Highly strung and loyal to those with whom he felt he had something to share, Webern remained close to Schoenberg but challenged him and often understood the full potential of his teacher's ideas before Schoenberg himself truly sensed their importance. Many years later, Webern apparently saw no contradiction between his deep loyalty to Schoenberg and his rather curious admiration for Hitler, even though his work as a composer became unacceptable to the Nazis, who classed it as 'degenerate'.

Other pupils, Heinrich Jalowetz, Paul Amadeus Pisk and Erwin Stein, all of whom would give Schoenberg invaluable support in the decades to come, developed their later careers as pianists, conductors and critics. Egon Wellesz, then Webern's close friend and fellow-student at the university, remained a problematic and uneasy follower, sometimes coming close to Schoenberg, sometimes drifting away; he was fascinated by Schoenberg, yet resisted the commitment and loyalty that Schoenberg came to expect from his students.

The house designed by Adolf Loos in Vienna for the Steiner family, at St Veit-Gasse 10. Schoenberg endorsed Loos's belief that a work of art had to be freed from all superficial ornamental detail.

A few months later this group was joined by Alban Berg, who was a little over a year younger than Webern. A cultured young man of refined musical and literary sensibility, vulnerable and constantly in need of encouragement, Berg provided a challenge for his teacher. Schoenberg said that when Berg came to him, his compositional approach extended no further than the melodic line of a lied with chordal accompaniment. But during the very early years of his apprenticeship Berg offered insights into his teacher's mind that proved invaluable. Better than anyone else at the time, Berg was able to analyse his teacher's music and provide explanatory notes for concert programmes and lectures, and to understand the intricacies of Schoenberg's orchestration. In the years that followed, Berg developed his own distinctive voice and acquired a mastery of musico-dramatic expression with less internal struggle than would be the case with Schoenberg when he came to write for the operatic stage in the 1920s. Unlike Wellesz, Berg was willing to submit to his teacher's requests for the preparation of piano scores, for running errands, and even for finding a removal firm when Schoenberg's belongings needed to be shipped from Vienna back to Berlin in 1911.

Schoenberg's magnetic personality, combined with his new status as teacher of a group of articulate pupils who were only some ten years or so younger than himself, contributed to his controversial reputation in Vienna, a city so conservative that it still regarded Mahler as a dangerously innovative composer. To the musical establishment Schoenberg was an iconoclast, while his pupils and several like-minded critics revered him. He became particularly close to Adolf Loos and was to hold him in high regard for the rest of his life. Loos's belief in the need to purge artistic expression of everything that was merely surface or ornamental, and to create designs that fitted their purpose, was the cornerstone of a new wave of architectural design in Vienna. Here the Haus Steiner and the Goldman and Salatsch department store eventually became iconic representations of modernity in architecture. With hindsight, we can observe the profound influence exerted on Schoenberg by Loos's stress on the economy of expressive means. For example, Loos's often-quoted dictum 'ornament is a sin' is paralleled by what Schoenberg had to say in 1949 about the formation of his own style of composition:

> ... the tendency to condense has gradually changed my entire style of composition ... by renouncing repetitions, sequences and elaboration, I finally arrived at a style of concision and brevity, in which every technical or structural necessity was carried out without unnecessary extension, in which every single unit is supposed to be functional.

In the first decade of the century Schoenberg was still some way away from this goal (he later judged that he reached it in the 1920s). His words here, as a description of the use of language, might well have come from Karl Kraus. In pre-1914 Vienna Kraus was the most vocal and probably the most influential critic of language at a time when a preoccupation with the limitations of language was a major theme in literature and philosophy. At the very beginning of the century several Austrians had voiced their distrust of traditional

Karl Kraus, c. 1909.
In his journal *Die Fackel*
('The Torch'), Kraus fought
for Modernist art and
against the misuse of
language by politicians
and populist journalists.

forms of expression. Philosopher Fritz Mauthner tried to unite the
clarity of the positivist Ernst Mach with a poetically charged belief
in the uniqueness of experience, arguing that any fixing in language
destroys that uniqueness. His *Beiträge zu einer Kritik der Sprache*
('Towards a Critique of Language', 1901–3) had a powerful impact
on Kraus and, a few years later, on Ludwig Wittgenstein, whose
Tractatus Logico-Philosophicus (1922) became a seminal work of
twentieth-century philosophy.

Hugo von Hofmannsthal had presented his doubts about language in a piece of masterly lyrical prose, bringing the philosophical
subject to a wide readership. *Ein Brief* ('A Letter'), as the piece was
entitled, appeared in the Berlin newspaper *Der Tag* in October 1902,
and if Schoenberg did not read it then, he almost certainly would
have done so later, for it became one of the crucial texts of Viennese
Modernism. In the letter Hofmannsthal projects himself into the
character of Lord Chandos, an Elizabethan courtier and poet, who

is purportedly writing to his former mentor Francis Bacon in 1603. Chandos informs Bacon that he has reached the limits of expression, that his creative power has been exhausted, and that his relationship with the world is now beset by an almost unbearable tension and sense of doubt. For Chandos, 'everything disintegrated into parts, those parts again into parts; no longer would anything let itself be encompassed by one idea. Single words floated round me; they congealed into eyes which stared at me and into which I was forced to stare back – whirlpools which gave me vertigo and, reeling incessantly, led into the void.' Through Chandos, Hofmannsthal offers a manifesto of alienation: a testimony that the innovations of the Symbolists, the insights of early psychoanalysis, and the profound revisions of hitherto accepted atomic theories had produced a spiritual vacuum. Chandos therefore declares that he will not write any more poetry, that language itself will have to be radically rethought, indeed, that a new 'angelic' language will have to be invented.

Unlike the resigned Chandos, Schoenberg showed a more positive will to continue with creative work. He recognized that the expressive richness such as he had achieved in *Pelleas und Melisande* would be difficult, if not impossible, to repeat. If the complexity and relatedness of motifs and themes, something that greatly interested him, was to be retained, it had to be achieved in a more condensed manner. In future, Schoenberg would often embark on a new work with the intention of overcoming or solving issues that an earlier work had raised. The cluster of finished works that followed *Pelleas*, from the years 1903 to 1906, included settings of poetry, and two chamber works – First String Quartet (1905) and First Chamber Symphony (1906) – which marked his coming of age as a composer and which in time would be recognized as classics of twentieth-century music. These known works are however only the tip of an iceberg whose submerged part consists of around twenty sketches for larger works. In some instances these sketches are of only a few bars' duration and point towards some ambitious project that was abandoned. It was not only Schoenberg's precarious financial circumstances that prevented these works from reaching completion. Self-criticism and a protracted struggle with the method of conceiving and sustaining large-scale works that employed increasingly complex harmonic and contrapuntal schemes were also important factors.

Setting poetry to music – Eight Songs with Piano Accompaniment, Op. 6, and Six Songs with Orchestral Accompaniment, Op. 8 – seems to have posed the fewest problems. Whereas the texts of Op. 6 show Schoenberg's continuing interest in contemporary German poets (Dehmel, John Henry Mackay, Friedrich Nietzsche), in Op. 8 his increasing admiration of Mahler is demonstrated by his choice of two poems from *Des Knaben Wunderhorn* ('The Boy's Magic Horn'), the collection of folk poetry to which Mahler repeatedly turned in the 1890s as his source. Nevertheless, it is Petrarch who, with three settings, dominates the set of six songs. Some years later Schoenberg admitted to Zemlinsky that two of the songs – *Natur* by Heinrich Hart and the German translation of Petrarch's *Nie ward ich, Herrin, müd* ('I have never been weary of loving you', No. 82 from the *Canzoniere*) – left him musically less satisfied. Although Mahler might have directed Schoenberg towards Petrarch, an additional stimulus might have been Schoenberg's reading of the nineteenth-century philosopher Arthur Schopenhauer: it was he who singled out Petrarch as the poet of that 'infinite yearning' which is to be found in erotic poetry. The desire to embrace high rhetorical register and the rarefied tone of 'pure' but erotically charged poetry would before long lead Schoenberg to Stefan George.

In December 1904 Mahler's Third Symphony was performed in Vienna for the first time and a few days later Schoenberg wrote enthusiastically to him:

And I believe I felt your symphony. I shared in the battling for illusion; I suffered the pangs of disillusionment; I saw the forces of evil and good wrestling with each other; I saw a man in torment struggling towards inner harmony; I divined a personality, a drama, and truthfulness, the most uncompromising truthfulness.

Interestingly, Schoenberg's sketchbook from this time contains an outline of a programme for his First String Quartet (his earlier string quartet of 1897 is not among his numbered quartets, and was only published in 1966). This outline – no more than a group of psychological 'moments' concerned with tension and transformation – was, as Schoenberg explained many years later, a private programme, and probably a leftover from the late Romantic aesthetic belief in musical narrative. Schoenberg was in fact already moving beyond a traditional type of musical narrative, towards a mode of musical thinking that favoured short motifs and phrases which were then elaborated through extensive reshaping and variation. In his later theoretical writings Schoenberg coined the term 'developing variation' to describe the process through which a melodic motif is elaborated to such an extent that it becomes only distantly related to its original shape – a process far removed from the obvious literal repetition so characteristic of the music from Haydn to Strauss and Mahler. Such a process accounts for the intensity of the First String Quartet and the difficulty it presented to the commentators and critics who tried to understand its one-movement form. Schoenberg had freed himself from the problems of texture and density experienced with *Pelleas*, and was now able to control the contrapuntal lines and allow them to retain their individuality, without the danger of their being swallowed by a large orchestral apparatus.

Some ten months separate the First String Quartet from the Chamber Symphony for fifteen solo instruments, Op. 9. In the hands of the late Romantics, the symphony had grown into a large and expansive multi-movement work, and once again Schoenberg seemed to want to make a statement, not only in response to Loos's ideas about restraint, but also by making more out of the economical use of instrumental timbres that Mahler had been exploring. In the Chamber Symphony the complexity of the one-movement form (already tried in the First String Quartet) is increased and fitted into the shorter time-span of only twenty minutes – around half the length of the quartet. The Chamber Symphony is tonal only in the sense that the key signature indicates E major. In reality, Schoenberg merely hints at the key of E here and there, only to dissolve it in highly chromatic episodes. It is the consistency of his reworking of motifs that ensures the continuity of seemingly disparate portions of the music. Each instrument behaves as a soloist and the old ideal of blending, characteristic of the Viennese symphonic style, is forsaken in favour of timbral contrasts. The impact was certainly novel then, but the passage of time has removed the Chamber Symphony's strangeness and it is now considered to be one of Schoenberg's accessible early works.

By employing an instrumental ensemble of ten wind players and only five strings, Schoenberg anticipated by some fifteen years the wind-dominated sound preferred by Stravinsky and Hindemith just after World War I. But in opting for contrasting sonorities he was not entirely without models to follow since, at the turn of the century, similar procedures began appearing in the works of composers whom we – from today's vantage point – would not consider radical innovators. When Mahler put on a new production of *La Bohème* in Vienna in 1904, Schoenberg and his pupils were particularly impressed by the contrasting timbres in Giacomo Puccini's orchestration, while another source of interesting ideas was Pfitzner's orchestration in the opera *Die Rose vom Liebesgarten*. Whereas Pfitzner, after an early progressive phase, became a chauvinist guardian of conservative virtues, and opposed to Schoenberg and his circle, Puccini, at first unaware of the impact he had made on the young Viennese composers, became in time an enthusiastic admirer of Schoenberg.

The Viennese critics remained, however, unwilling to consider anything that transgressed the boundaries of the late Romantic idiom. Accordingly, the gap of only a few days between the first performances of the First String Quartet and that of the First Chamber Symphony in February 1907 meant that the critics' fury was all the more intense. The quartet provoked the derogatory term 'Secessionist' from the influential newspaper critic Julius Korngold (father of the child-prodigy composer Erich Wolfgang Korngold), while the Chamber Symphony divided the audience. Schoenberg's friends tried to counter the whistling and shouting of the hostile audience with their expressions of enthusiasm. At the performance of the quartet, Mahler tried to impose his authority, only to be told: 'We whistle at the performances of your symphonies too!' After the performance of the Chamber Symphony, Hans Liebstöckl reported in the *Illustriertes Wiener Extra-Blatt* that 'Herr Hofoperndirector Gustav Mahler, who has headed for some time now the protectorate of degenerate [*entartete*] music, was standing in one of the boxes, pale and with his lips tightly pressed together' – thereby claiming one of the early uses of the term of censure for avant-garde art, *entartete*, that was later adopted by the Nazis.

The stormy reception of the two new works signalled the beginning of a particularly stressful period in Schoenberg's life, which was to last for around four years. Whereas his later crises, particularly at the time of his flight from Europe after the Nazi seizure of power in

Germany, were more external in their origin, the one looming in 1907
derived from the animosities generated by his work in Vienna and
a fraught personal situation. He was particularly vulnerable because
his energy was also being sapped by a self-imposed insistence on
planning each new work as a means to improve on some aspects
of earlier pieces which he felt had been inadequately handled.

The first completed work following the concerts of 1907 was a
choral setting of *Friede auf Erden* ('Peace on Earth'), an especially
poignant poem by the late nineteenth-century Swiss poet Conrad
Ferdinand Meyer. Although the choral texture distantly recalls
Bach's and Brahms's motets, the dissonant harmonies add to the
music's expressive force. Its composition coincided with the first
sketches for a new string quartet and a new chamber symphony.
The sound-world of the quartet is brimming with tensions which,
as will be seen later, were far more complex than mere straightforward reflections of difficult life experiences. Schoenberg had
been plagued by the uncertainties of everyday existence for some
time now, and the arrival of a second child, Georg, also known as
Görgi, in September 1906 put even more pressure on him to provide
for his family. Although poverty was a continuing feature of
Schoenberg's family life, certain aspects of a normal Viennese existence continued – for example, holidays in the country, usually by an
Alpine lake. The First Chamber Symphony had been completed
during just such a holiday at Rottach-Egern, in Bavaria, even though
the summer of 1906 had been overshadowed by news of the death of
Maria Mahler, Alma's and Gustav's older daughter. Schoenberg, who
like many Viennese of that time subscribed to both rational and
irrational modes of perception, sank into a particularly self-searching
mode. Little is known about the intimate details of his family life,
but it seems likely that Mathilde Schönberg suffered from postnatal
depression after the birth of her second child. Friends relate that the
once vivacious woman withdrew into herself more and more, and
Schoenberg's preoccupation with creative matters could well have
exacerbated the creeping alienation from his wife.

In spring 1907 Schoenberg interrupted work on the new string
quartet to compose Two Ballads for Voice and Piano, Op. 12. In the
summer he started sketching the Second Chamber Symphony,
leaving it as no more than a torso that he would complete, but only

The Laughing Man –
Richard Gerstl's self-portrait,
1908, painted at the time of
his brief affair with Mathilde
Schönberg. The emotional
force of Gerstl's painting
made him a forerunner of
Expressionism in Austria.

after a fashion, decades later. Finally, between December 1907 and
February 1908 he completed Two Songs, Op. 14. Mahler's resignation
from the Court Opera and departure for New York in December
1907, in the face of increasing vilification from the musical establishment, only increased Schoenberg's vulnerability. He turned to
painting partly as a form of therapy, and partly as an additional
way of tackling the wider problems of language and of expression.

   Schoenberg's painting was a form of instantaneous expression and
consisted of bursts of pent-up spiritual energy. The little help that
he received in mastering the technique of brushwork came from
Richard Gerstl, a rebellious and highly strung young man who was
searching equally frantically for original painterly expression. Gerstl
had been befriended by the Schoenbergs in the period before the
concerts of February 1907 and they subsequently became neighbours
in the Lichtensteinstrasse, where Gerstl hired a studio. At the time
Schoenberg seems to have been battling on two fronts: his composing
and his marriage. In early 1908 he again turned to the highly rarefied
poetry of Stefan George, which he had first encountered through the

Portrait of Mathilde and
Trudi Schönberg by
Richard Gerstl, 1906. The
painting was made close to
the time of the photograph
on page 37.

concerts of the Ansorge Society. George's exquisite attention to poetic
form and his incantatory use of language rendered him a legend-
ary figure, a sage-like poetic Arthur presiding over a Camelot of
poetic disciples. His poetry answered Schoenberg's need for purity
of intention and execution, and the composer proceeded to clothe
the poems in musical textures of concentrated complexity, thereby
bringing together Loos's ideal of conciseness with his own urge to
express himself in a language springing from pure intuition. It is
easy to imagine that immersion in such an intuitively creative process
went hand in hand with self-absorption. It was probably Mathilde's
depression and increased loneliness that caused her to turn to Gerstl
and it was not long before Schoenberg's daughter reported to her
father that she had seen Mathilde and Gerstl kissing. In June 1908
Mathilde, her mother and the children left to spend the summer
by lake Traunsee, while Schoenberg stayed in Vienna. An intense
correspondence followed, with Mathilde denying a relationship with
Gerstl; nevertheless, Gerstl appeared at Traunsee only a day after
Schoenberg joined his family there.

Schoenberg by Gerstl, 1906. Schoenberg took up painting at this time, but later denied he had been in any way influenced by Gerstl or Kokoschka.

It is often claimed that aspects of the Second String Quartet were shaped by the affair, but it would be truer to say that Mathilde's relationship with Gerstl interacted with the dynamics of the composition without drastically altering a work that was already planned. Schoenberg conceived the quartet in separate movements, rather than in the one-movement form that he had favoured until then, although the cyclic character is retained, since material from the first movement reappears later in the quartet. The second movement, a grim scherzo, quotes, in a somewhat Mahlerian manner, a popular song: 'O my dearest Augustin, everything's lost.' This is often interpreted as a reference to the marital crisis, although a jotting in a sketchbook indicates that Schoenberg had thought of it earlier.

Unusually, the quartet departs from the pure instrumental spirit of chamber music in its third and fourth movements, where a solo soprano is introduced. Schoenberg had requested from his friend Karl Horwitz copies of two of George's poems from his recently published anthology *Der siebente Ring* ('The Seventh Ring') and received them a few days after his arrival at Traunsee. Setting these

poems for soprano and quartet – which occupied him for a few
months – was indeed done in the thick of the worsening marital crisis,
which culminated in Mathilde leaving the family and moving, first
to Gmünden and then to Vienna. Although it is easy to read in his
choice of poems a reflection of that situation, Schoenberg had in fact
made his selection some time before. Schoenberg was close to being
obsessed with George's poetry and yet there is a deep contradiction
between the intentions of the two men. In *Der siebente Ring* George
had sought to give poetic expression to an atmosphere of refinement
and reflection, inspired by the death of a young man who had
captured the imagination of George's homosexual circle. Schoenberg,
in contrast, was searching for a way of shaping intuitive expression
within a unique musical texture for which such an elevated poetic
idiom as George's would provide a suitable framework. This was in
part achieved through a texture in which, in keeping with George's
line 'Ich löse mich in Tönen' ('I am being dissolved in sounds'),
traditional harmonic language gives way to a rich succession of
moments in which dissonance and consonance appear as equal.
The image of musical texture as a living, constantly changing
'organic' structure was by then in any case an accepted mode of
thinking in music theory, and soon the increased importance
given to dissonances became reflected in the phrase 'the emancipation of dissonance' – where a dissonance no longer resolves
onto a consonance as a matter of course.

Stefan George's 'Ich fühle Luft von anderem Planeten' ('I feel the
air from other-worldly spheres'), the opening image of the poem
which Schoenberg set in the final movement of the quartet, is less
an evocation of the poet's aloofness or the composer's portrayal
of a marital crisis than a statement of Schoenberg's desire to break
through the gravitational pull of a tonal centre, something that
had occupied him for quite some time before his domestic troubles.
Some critics claimed that this fourth movement was the first of
Schoenberg's compositions to be written without a key signature,
in a style of high chromaticism that would eventually be called
'atonal'. This term signifies both the absence of a clear tonal centre,
and the suspension of traditional tonal process depending on tensions and resolutions – the 'emancipation of dissonance' was here in
full spate. In fact, in the quartet movement Schoenberg was only

extending the idiom which he had started to develop early in 1908 when he began setting the first in a group of fifteen poems from George's collection *Die Bücher der Hirten- und Preisgedichte, der Sagen und Sänge, und der hängenden Gärten* ('The Books of Eclogues and Eulogies, of Legends and Lays, and the Hanging Gardens', 1895). In these George sought to shape his poetry in exquisite patterns in which every detail was carefully controlled, and the conciseness of each poem, as well as a high poetic register, was particularly attractive to Schoenberg. Schoenberg's aim of creating musical miniatures controlled from within, through a succession of chordal and melodic kernels stretching over a short span of intensely chromatic music, governed by the 'developing variation' and not by restatement, went against George's aim of imposing an overall form on the poems. Instead, Schoenberg gave them a new, expression-governed reading, lending them in the process a dimension that George's poetry lacked.

By late September 1908 Mathilde, broken, but also persuaded by Webern's pleas, had returned to the family and the affair was brought to an end by Gerstl's gruesome suicide in November. He had simultaneously hanged and stabbed himself, after having destroyed several of his canvases. As a painter, he remained unknown until 1933 when an exhibition of his surviving paintings was held in Vienna. But his memory lived on in the minds of those who had been so powerfully affected by him, and for as long as the Schoenbergs lived in Vienna they visited his grave on the anniversary of his suicide.

The score of Schoenberg's Second String Quartet was published with a simple dedication: 'To my wife.' At the first public performance, in December 1908, recent history repeated itself, as if the tensions surrounding the work's gestation had spilled over into the concert hall. The Rosé Quartet and the soprano Marie Gutheil-Schoder were met with such laughter and protests from the audience that the work could not be properly heard. The distressed Gutheil-Schoder fled to Bertha Zuckerkandl's house and had to be calmed down. The quartet, nowadays considered to be one of Schoenberg's more accessible works, met with little comprehension and the conservative critic Ludwig Karpath said that his review of the première belonged not to the paper's arts section but to the chronicle of local scandals. Both he and his fellow-critic Max Kalbeck described the quartet as 'music of the cats'. Even Arthur Schnitzler, by no means

inimical to new art, recorded in his diary: 'I do not believe in
Schoenberg. I understood Bruckner and Mahler straight away, do
I have to fail now?' Kraus and Loos, on the other hand, supported
Schoenberg above all because what they had witnessed confirmed
the strength of personal conviction and the importance of adhering
to one's artistic principles.

Schnitzler's apparent failure to comprehend Schoenberg should not
be dismissed as the erroneous opinion of someone who had not seen
the light, for he seemed to sense that Schoenberg made his audience
listen according to different criteria. In poetic and rhetorical terms
the criteria were referred to by later commentators and critics, notably
Egon Wellesz and Theodor Wiesengrund Adorno, as 'truth' and
'necessity', and this chimed in with the views of Loos and Kraus.
In addition, in technical terms the music demanded an instantaneous
involvement and an ability to recognize the interactions between
different dimensions, harmonic and contrapuntal. This involved
an analytical faculty with which wider audiences were not equipped.
Igor Stravinsky and Béla Bartók would eventually expect a similar
commitment from their listeners, but Schoenberg was the first
to make such a demand, and he provoked in the process a reaction
which tended to demonize him. It also created around him
an atmosphere of rejection that would follow him in later life.

4

Schoenberg in Alexander
Siloti's fur coat,
St Petersburg, 1912.

Necessity creates form. *Fish that live at great
depths have no eyes. The elephant has a trunk.
The chameleon changes its colour, etc. etc.
Form reflects the spirit of the individual artist.
Form bears the stamp of the* personality.

Wassily Kandinsky,
'On the Question of Form',
Der Blaue Reiter Almanac, 1912

Heroes, Clowns and Beasts 1908–14

'Of the two of us Richard had chosen for himself the easier way,'
Mathilde wrote to Alois Gerstl after his brother's suicide, and this
rather grim admission indicates that the tensions that had come to
a head in the summer of 1908 had left a deep scar on the Schoenberg
family. Much later, in 1934, soon after his arrival in the USA,
Schoenberg expressed his long-suppressed resentment, referring to
Gerstl as a person who had 'invaded' his house, while playing down
the 'invader's' role as his instructor in the technique of painting.
Once the affair was over, friends and pupils saw that Schoenberg
had drawn a veil over it and, indeed, it was overshadowed by continuing battles over artistic principles. The view has often been
expressed that Schoenberg's artistic progress was something auton-
omous, resting on ideals alone and having nothing to do with
the mundane aspects of existence. While it is true that Schoenberg
tended to suppress the mundane, he also tended to sublimate
chaotic everyday experience into an ordered process, and this
seemed to generate the energy that he needed when interacting
with his surroundings – which he saw in terms of a battle.

In some respects, Schoenberg resembled the Romantic polymath
E. T. A. Hoffmann. Although Hoffmann left a slight impact as
a composer, he was an able painter and, as a critic and essayist,
he profoundly influenced music criticism in nineteenth-century
Germany. Schoenberg too was drawn to poetry, critical prose and
painting, and in addition, displayed a post-Wagnerian yearning
towards a fusion of the arts. Wagner's excursions into stage and
theatre design provided Schoenberg with a model, but on the whole
Schoenberg was less innovative in this area and set greater store by
his activity as a painter. If painting began for Schoenberg as a means
of dealing with inner psychological turmoil, it was soon elevated to
a more significant process of artistic syncretism, while the written
word enabled him to engage with his critics and realize some of his
literary aspirations.

The tenacity that Schoenberg showed in pursuing these various
activities allowed him to explore the intellectual currents that surrounded him and to detect the affinities between other contemporary
artists and himself. During the period between his first songs and
the First String Quartet he was still close to *fin-de-siècle* aesthetics,
learning from people like Jacobsen, Dehmel, Klimt, Bahr and
Strauss, who were themselves searching for new modes of expression.
While musical composition was one way of proceeding, the written
word and painting became increasingly important to him. After the
stormy reception of the Second String Quartet, he felt that he ought
to respond to the intemperate critic Ludwig Karpath, and when
no Viennese paper wanted to publish his open letter, Karl Kraus
eventually included it in *Die Fackel*. Despite his lack of musical understanding, Kraus continued to defend Schoenberg since he believed
that his supreme task was to ensure the right of an artist to express
himself. Kraus urged Schoenberg not to address his critics in an
impersonal and generalized way, but to consider them as individuals
with whose ideas he had to engage directly. Schoenberg took this
advice and in his later writings he frequently fired salvoes at his
perceived opponents. Unfortunately, this approach also created difficulties in his relationships with some of his contemporaries such as
Stravinsky, the conductor Otto Klemperer and, above all, the writer
Thomas Mann.

Schoenberg's work in early 1909 is a telling illustration of his search
for new modes of expression. *Das Buch der hängenden Gärten* ('The
Book of the Hanging Gardens') was finished early in that year, completing the chronological frame around the Second String Quartet.
But although the songs and quartet share some of the harmonic language that has been freed from tonal structures, they in fact represent
two distinct tendencies. The quartet adheres to the tradition of expansive lines and cyclic unity in which motivic elements of one
movement appear in another. The songs, though unified poetically,
tend to complete a musical statement within the frame of a miniature, with the miniatures succeeding one another without developing
a broad narrative pattern. Schoenberg now faced the challenge of
extending the free, atonal style of the George songs to instrumental
works, where the music alone would regulate the compositional
process. The term 'atonal', used to describe a harmonic system

without a key signature and without standard triadic patterns, leading
to recognizable cadential points of closure, was disliked by Schoenberg,
who proposed instead a descriptive phrase: 'composition with twelve
notes related only to one another.' Nevertheless, 'atonality' has
remained in use (even if, etymologically, it does not suit music that
depends on a progression of notes, or 'tones').

Schoenberg wrote the music for the last George song and the two
initial Piano Pieces from Op. 11 in February and March 1909, and
the speed with which he completed these complex compositions is
astonishing given that he had no models to follow for the Piano
Pieces other than the textures of the piano accompaniment to the
George songs. As we have seen, Schoenberg was not a pianist and this
may have actually helped him. He was not tempted to opt for tested
patterns, whereas a trained pianist would have reached for figurations
and passages almost instinctively.

The goal of the early Expressionist poets, such as Georg Kaiser
and Ernst Stadler, may have been to capture the 'inner essence' of
poetic utterance and trance – or dream-like bursts of energy. But
their poetry still contained concepts and grammatical constructions
that linked it with everyday language. Conversely, the radical
'musicalization' of poetry and near-abandonment of discursive
language would be attempted by the Dada poets a few years later.
Schoenberg realized that as a composer he was in a privileged
position because the non-referential nature of music removes any
residual link with conceptually framed meaning. This he set out
to explore in the Piano Pieces, Op. 11. At first they strike the listener
as collections of unrelated 'events'. But in fact they present a succession of motivic cells that assume the functions of chords and
melodic shards but without adhering to a pattern that the listener's
mind can anticipate. Such a texture does not rely on the regular
phrase-lengths and repetitions found in the music of the late eighteenth and nineteenth centuries, and Schoenberg coined for it the
term 'musical prose'. He was quite clear about his intentions, and
in a letter of August 1909 to Ferruccio Busoni, to whom he had sent
the first two pieces the month before, he explained his aesthetic
position in a piece of prose which, even in its layout, has affinities
with the typography of Dada:

I strive for: complete liberation from all forms
from all symbols
of cohesion and
of logic.
  Thus:
away with 'motivic working out.'
Away with harmony as
cement or bricks of a building.
  Harmony is expression
and nothing else.
  Then:
Away with Pathos!
Away with protracted ten-ton scores, from erected or constructed
towers, rocks and other massive claptrap.
My music must be
brief.
Concise! In two notes: not built, but 'expressed'!!

Ferruccio Busoni, painting by Max Oppenheimer, 1916. A composer and a celebrated pianist, Busoni offered Schoenberg much-needed support in Berlin.

Webern later remarked that the form of the pieces emerges from within and that the reiteration of motivic references and of certain pivotal pitches do provide points of articulation. Their textures invite comparison with Debussy's stripping down of rich chordal sonorities in favour of individual notes, but it is difficult to establish how far Schoenberg was aware of Debussy's idiom at the time since his own testimony is contradictory. In 1936, commenting on the manuscript of Willi Reich's biography of Berg, Schoenberg wrote that he had not known Debussy's music during the years when Berg was studying with him, but this goes against what Schoenberg had said about Debussy in an interview with Paul Wilhelm in 1909. In any case, Debussy's frequent use of unvaried or little-varied repetitions would not have appealed to Schoenberg.

Busoni's response to the two pieces from Op. 11 was very encouraging and his criticism was limited to suggested changes that would make the pieces 'more pianistic'. It is a measure of Schoenberg's trust in Busoni that he did not react with his customary rashness – rather, he responded with a carefully argued explanation of his own aesthetic position, thus initiating an important correspondence that lasted throughout 1909. At about the same time, Schoenberg demonstrated his confidence in his own path by adding a third piece to the set.

The exchange of letters with Busoni came just after Schoenberg had also completed the Five Orchestral Pieces, Op. 16. He started working on these short but extremely complex compositions in May 1909, and completed the orchestration by mid August. Just as Op. 11 was an essay in condensed musical argument, so the Five Orchestral Pieces sought to produce the opposite of the symphonic length and elaborate development which were then the norm. The kind of development encountered here consists of the unfolding of several densely argued thematic fragments, which achieve the intensity and richness of standard symphonic movements in a short space of time. Although the Five Orchestral Pieces carry descriptive titles, these titles owe their existence to the publishers Peters and were, in Schoenberg's words, to be understood only as 'technical'. The orchestra that he deployed contrasted markedly with the brevity of the pieces, allowing the richness of timbral combinations to emerge in full. Nowhere is this so clearly achieved as in No. 3, *Farben* ('Colours'), in which seamless instrumental shadings vary the same

something which may be the corpse of her lover. Nothing is revealed –
the Woman may be imagining it all, and the encounter with the
corpse may even be a projection of her own state of mind. In the
parlance of the time this was a case of 'hysteria', a condition accorded
social and intellectual importance by Sigmund Freud and Joseph
Breuer's 1895 study. Based on the analysis of a subject called Anna O.
(a woman who may have been related to Marie Pappenheim), the
study claimed that psychic trauma and its accompanying emotions
became a 'foreign body' in the psyche that was inaccessible to
normal consciousness, but emerged in therapy under hypnosis.
A further twist to this theory was given in Otto Weininger's widely
read, pseudo-scientific study *Geschlecht und Charakter* ('Sex and
Character', 1903), in which he combined Freudian ideas with the
theories of Count Gobineau, thus providing sustenance to anti-
Semitism, racial theories and misogyny. Schoenberg had already
discovered the concepts of alienation and misogyny through his
fascination with Strindberg, and this was only reinforced with
his contacts with Kraus, who, though critical of Freud, believed in
Weininger. Pappenheim herself may not have been influenced
by Weininger, while Schoenberg, receptive to a range of influences,
was open to both Freud and Weininger.

The non-repetitive, stream-of-consciousness music of *Erwartung*
offers the musical equivalent of a hysteric's state of mind. It created
an immediacy which no previous music drama had possessed; its
concluding passage – a run of chromatic scales in contrary motion
that come to a precipitous end without any semblance of a musical
cadence – seems to flow directly into the listener's consciousness.
Even more than when Pappenheim created her share of the work –
poetry brimming with references to the surrounding objects (wood,
trees) and apparitions and symbols interpreted by a deranged mind
(blood-red moon, swaying moon) – Schoenberg's composing process
flowed as though he were in a trance, and the short score was completed between 27 August and 12 September, with the final phase
of the orchestration taking only three more weeks. Theodor
Wiesengrund Adorno later summed up *Erwartung* as the 'infinity
of a second compressed into 400 bars'. The score would be published
in 1916, but nothing came of several early attempts to put on a performance. At first, the need for a large orchestra was the obstacle, and

Schoenberg's portrait of
Marie Pappenheim, 1909.
At that time she wrote the
text for *Erwartung*.

Oskar Kokoschka and
Herwarth Walden in Berlin,
c. 1912. Kokoschka is
holding a copy of the
periodical Der Sturm
('The Storm') which Walden
founded in 1910 as a forum
for avant-garde literature
and art.

then the outbreak of World War I further delayed the work's
première. When Zemlinsky eventually conducted it for the first
time, in Prague in 1924, it had a retrospective feel about it since
the main wave of German Expressionism, of which the work is
such a poignant example, had already passed.

An important part of Expressionist aesthetics was the conviction
that the intense translation of an inner vision into a form removes
the distinction between the arts – hence the pursuit of several artistic media by a number of the Expressionists. In Vienna, Oskar
Kokoschka moved from painting to literature, while in Berlin
Herwarth Walden sought to unite painters, composers and poets by
means of the periodical Der Sturm ('The Storm') and its attendant
institutions. A similar programme was pursued in Munich by the
painter Wassily Kandinsky. Throughout 1907 and 1908 Schoenberg

had been increasingly attracted to painting, and after the Gerstl
affair the need to express himself through the medium became even
more urgent. Human faces interested him above all: friends, family
and, repeatedly, self-portraits – a telling sign that for him painting
was a way of self-exploration. Later, Schoenberg was eager to stress
that he had been self-taught and free from direct influences, even
accusing Wellesz and Paul Stefan of 'spreading a lie' that he had been
influenced by Kokoschka. During 1908 and 1909 he produced a series
of paintings that forsook the straightforward representation of a face
and concentrated on the flaming eyes – these he called 'gazes'. He
was here painting an image encountered in contemporary prose and
poetry. Hofmannsthal's Chandos, for instance, experiences words
dissolving and becoming gazing eyes, an image which Pappenheim
incorporates also into *Erwartung*. Similarly, in the paintings of Emil
Nolde and other Expressionist portrait painters the eyes are often the
most prominent feature of the human face. But Schoenberg's expressive intention was stronger than his mastery of the technique of
painting. This primacy of the expressive urge impressed the radical
Kandinsky, but the paintings disappointed the more conservative
August Macke, who, in a letter to Franz Marc, described
Schoenberg's faces as 'green-eyed bread-rolls'.

At a particularly desperate moment, in March 1910, Schoenberg
wrote to the publisher Emil Hertzka; he saw no future for himself
as a composer who could earn his living, he said, and asked Hertzka
to help him become established as a portrait painter. Schoenberg
was, however, already at work on his book on the theory of harmony,
Harmonielehre, and the strength of the intellectual commitment
required overpowered the more escapist idea of painting to order.
An exhibition of Schoenberg's paintings in the Heller bookshop in
Vienna in October 1910 was, predictably, a mixed success. The critics
were unimpressed and on 14 October Schnitzler noted in his diary
that Schoenberg's talent was undetectable. But some paintings were
sold and he earned a fee. After Mahler's death the following year,
Webern told Schoenberg that the buyer had in fact been Mahler
(Schoenberg had turned to his fellow-composer for financial help
earlier in 1910, promptly receiving the sum of 800 kronen).

The reception of the *Harmonielehre*, published in 1911 by Hertzka's
Universal Edition, provided one source of encouragement. The hefty

Opposite, Schoenberg's *Red Gaze,* May 1910, oil on cardboard. The directness of painterly expression impressed Wassily Kandinsky, while August Macke called a similar picture by Schoenberg a 'green-eyed bread-roll'.

Left, Schoenberg's self-portraits from 1910, oil on wood. The face is suggested through its essential features, the eyes being particularly prominent, as in most Expressionist portraits. Schoenberg's repeated returns to self-portraits suggest that for him painting was a form of self-analysis.

volume bore a dedication 'to the hallowed memory of Gustav Mahler';
it established Schoenberg as a formidable music theorist and has
remained a classic. Uninformed critics have often assumed that the
book was a theoretical manifesto of atonality. It was nothing of
the kind – it was a carefully thought-out discussion of the principles
of harmonic practice until around 1900 and contained searching
thoughts on the nature of creativity. Traditionally, books on harmony
tended to spell out 'rules' of 'correct' writing, but Schoenberg
saw these as attempts by dogmatic theorists to divorce theory from
creativity; his own professed aim was to explain the logic underpinning the harmonic practice of tonal music and the need for
a constant evolution of harmonic language. Not uncharacteristically,
he soon became dissatisfied with some of his original formulations
and produced a revised version, which was published in 1922.

Opposite,
Schoenberg's design
for whist/bridge cards,
1910. One of several
sets designed by him.

Expressionist many-sidedness, involving Schoenberg the poet,
the stage designer and the composer, is revealed to the full in a
stage work that was conceived in 1910 – the drama with music *Die
glückliche Hand* ('The Lucky Hand' or 'The Knack'). *Erwartung*
had suggested that a rival had estranged the lover from the protagonist, but this similarity to the love triangle involving Gerstl
was most likely just a coincidence since the text was Pappenheim's
idea. *Die glückliche Hand* was, however, autobiographical, and
Schoenberg may have been inspired by the imagery of the opening
of Hofmannsthal's enigmatic poem *Die Beiden* ('The Two'), which
he had set to music in 1899.

The action of *Die glückliche Hand* is pared down to bare essentials:
the Man encounters the Woman (a silent role), who hands him a
goblet. The Man drinks from it, and the Woman disappears just
as the Man believes that he is embracing her. The Man wanders,
the Woman reappears, half-naked, with the missing part of her
dress held by a Gentleman (another silent role). She then turns into
a menacing spectre and pushes a stone, which falls on the Man
and buries him. The chorus of six men and six women, the same
ensemble that was heard at the beginning of the work, then sings
the moral which concludes with the lines:

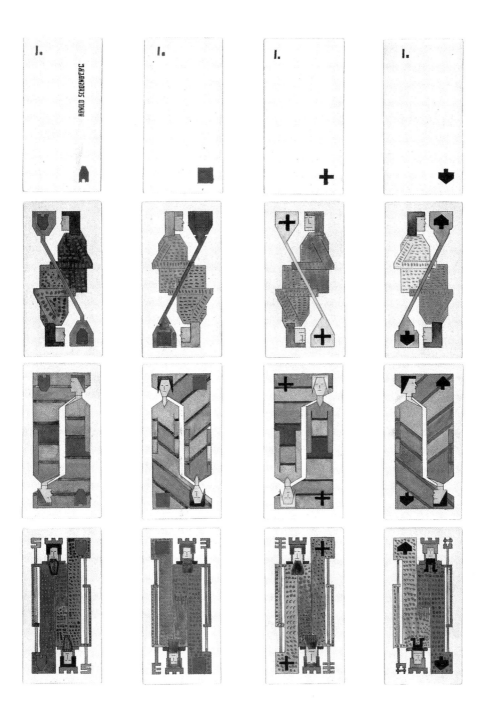

Anton Webern (left) and
Schoenberg in a Berlin
street, in the 1920s. Of all
his pupils Webern was
closest to Schoenberg and
one of the few whom
Schoenberg allowed to
address him with the familiar
form of 'du'.

And still you seek!
And torment yourself!
And are without rest!
You poor soul!

The work was completed in Berlin in 1913, but its roots lie firmly in
the time when Schoenberg was intensely preoccupied with painting;
the colours of the décor and the intricate lighting are integral to the
work and may have been suggested by Kokoschka's handling of these

Oskar Kokoschka, *Pietà*,
1909 – poster for his play
*Mörder, Hoffnung der
Frauen* ('Murderer, Hope
of Women').

devices in his 1907 play *Mörder, Hoffnung der Frauen* ('Murderer,
Hope of Women'). Schoenberg succeeded in producing a 'total work
of art' that goes beyond Kandinsky's abstract drama *Der gelbe Klang*
('The Yellow Sound', 1909–12), since Kandinsky was no composer
and the work's score (now lost) was written by the Russian composer
Thomas von Hartmann.

Die glückliche Hand derived some additional sustenance from
Schoenberg's association with artists in Berlin and Munich, which
began shortly after he started working on the score in September
1910. Once more the lure of Germany, especially Berlin, as a place
where his art would be appreciated, counterbalanced the depression
that left so many traces throughout 1910. Only three weeks after
his exhibition of paintings opened in the Salon at the Heller
bookshop, Schoenberg went to Berlin to attend a performance of
his *Pelleas und Melisande,* conducted by Oskar Fried. Webern, who
was now working in a small theatre (like so many other aspiring

conductors), came across from Danzig. There were to be many
occasions when Schoenberg's devoted pupils would accompany their
teacher as if in an act of personal homage, turning the performance
into an act of collective admiration and affirmation of belief.

Opposite,
Some members of the *Blaue
Reiter* group in Munich,
c. 1911: Maria and Franz
Marc, Bernhard Koehler,
Wassily Kandinsky (seated),
Heinrich Campendonk and
Thomas von Hartmann.

Schoenberg's direct contact with artists in Munich was established
in January 1911 when Kandinsky, Gabriele Münter, Franz Marc,
Alexander von Jawlensky and Marianne von Werefkin attended
a concert of his works there – piano music and songs, plus a performance of both quartets by Rosé's ensemble. Kandinsky and his
friends were at the time amongst the radical members of the group
Die Neue Künstlervereinigung München or NKVM ('The New
Artists' Association of Munich'), united in their search for ways
of expressing an 'inner vision' without regard for convention or
representationalism. The enthusiasm they felt on experiencing
Schoenberg's music was summed up by Marc in a letter to Macke
on 11 January 1911:

> *Some music I heard in Munich gave me a real jolt; chamber music
> by Arnold Schönberg (Vienna). Two quartets, piano pieces, and songs
> … Can you imagine music in which tonality (that is, retention of any key)
> is completely abandoned? Listening to that music, I kept thinking of
> Kandinsky's large composition, which hasn't any tonality either …
> Schönberg works on the principle that consonance and dissonance don't
> exist at all. So-called dissonance is only a consonance which has been
> stretched. I am really preoccupied with this idea in painting …*

Marc's description may not be the best guide to Schoenberg's aesthetics but it is a potent illustration of the feeling of kinship which
members of the Munich avant garde experienced on encountering
his music. Kandinsky – who in 1910 was still painting in a semi-
figurative manner, but moving ever nearer to abstraction – sensed
that Schoenberg's atonal style was proof that intense expression
could be achieved by using a language which radically departed
from established conventions. On 18 January 1911 he wrote to
Schoenberg, introducing himself and explaining the closeness of
their respective positions:

In your works, you have realized what I, albeit in uncertain form, have so greatly longed for in music. The independent progress through their own destinies, the independent life of the individual voices in your compositions, is exactly what I am trying to find in my paintings.

Kandinsky and Schoenberg first met during the summer of 1911, when the composer was staying on the Starnberger See, not far from Murnau, the Bavarian village in which Kandinsky had settled with

Münter in 1909. At the end of 1911 Kandinsky and the radical members of the NKVM, increasingly dissatisfied with the more conservative wing, broke away, and established the group known as *Der Blaue Reiter* ('The Blue Rider'). The meeting between Kandinsky and Schoenberg was the beginning of an intense artistic friendship which, like so many of Schoenberg's relationships, had its highs and lows. It also led directly to Schoenberg's involvement with *Der Blaue Reiter* and to the publication of his first clear statement of his aesthetic position, the essay *Das Verhältnis zum Text* ('Relationship to the Text'), in the *Der Blaue Reiter* Almanac in 1912. The essay opens in a very decisive manner:

There are relatively few people who are capable of understanding, purely in terms of music, what music has to say. The assumption that a piece of music must summon up images of one sort or another, and that if these are absent the piece of music has not been understood or is worthless, is as widespread as only the false and banal can be. Nobody expects such a thing from any other art but rather contents himself with the effects of the material.

Kandinsky, *Lyrisches* ('Lyrically'), woodcut after his 1911 oil painting of the same title. Horsemen had been Kandinsky's favourite motif since 1903; here, the horse is still recognizable, but its rider is reduced to an abstract form, in keeping with Kandinsky's desire to achieve an expressive effect through the association of colour and line. The painting was executed only a few days after Kandinsky attended the concert of Schoenberg's music.

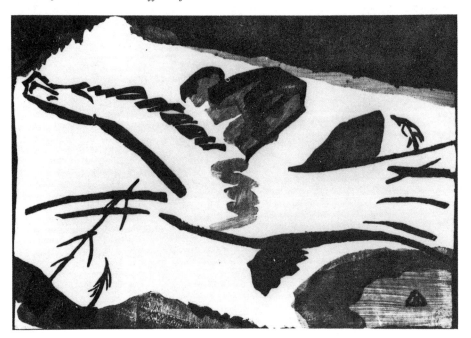

In 1936 Kandinsky reminded Schoenberg of the circumstances of their first meeting:

Do you still remember, dear Mr Schönberg, how we met – I arrived on the steamer wearing short Lederhosen and saw a black-and-white graphic – you were dressed completely in white and only your face was deeply tanned. And later, the summer in Murnau? All our contemporaries from that time sigh deeply when they remember that vanished epoch and say: 'That was a beautiful time'. And it really was beautiful, more than beautiful. How wonderfully life pulsated then, what quick spiritual triumphs we expected. Even today I expect them, and with the most complete certainty. But I know that a long, long time will still be necessary.

The times were by no means beautiful, but Kandinsky's nostalgia was not uncritical, and when he was remembering the summer of 1911 from the perspective of the 1930s, the freshness of the artistic innovation that was then so much a part of their lives looked particularly meaningful.

With Mahler's death on 18 May 1911 in Vienna, Schoenberg lost a protector and a friend who, despite being at the mercy of the Viennese cliques, had always been ready to stand up for him. Schoenberg's response was a poignant musical statement, a composition comprising only nine bars of sparse sonorities. This was added, as the sixth and last piece, to a group of five pieces written in February. The Six Little Piano Pieces, Op. 19, were the last compositions that Schoenberg would complete in Vienna before he left for Berlin a second time.

In 1911 his Viennese environment had changed rapidly. Webern had married his cousin Wilhelmine Mörtl in February. Berg's marriage to Helene Nahowski followed in May and Schoenberg must have felt, without justification as it turned out, that his close circle of friends and pupils was dissolving. Both he and Mathilde were experiencing bad health; Mahler's death made the horizon appear even darker; and, to cap it all, there was an unpleasant confrontation with a neighbour, who threatened Schoenberg and accused his ten-year-old daughter of making advances to his young son. Schoenberg was particularly upset by this incident and saw it as the epitome of all the artistic opposition he was facing in Vienna.

Alban Berg (seated) looking up to his teacher. The body language reveals the high esteem in which he always held Schoenberg.

In a letter to Schoenberg, Berg, too, equated the animosity of the public with the actions of the irascible neighbour: 'Is this not rather [the] fulfilment of the fate of genius? Regardless [of] whether manifested negatively, in the incomprehension of a thousand "sensible" people, or positively, in the hatred of a madman!'

Schoenberg had arrived back in Berlin by late September 1911, even though his future was by no means certain and his financial position as precarious as ever. It may be that his hopes had been raised by Kandinsky, who had good contacts with Herwarth Walden in Berlin. Otherwise, Schoenberg relied on Edward Clark, a young Englishman then studying in Berlin and writing for *The Musical Times*, and on Busoni, who assured him that composition pupils would be eagerly awaiting him. By now Schoenberg had the reputation of being an inspiring and demanding teacher, and this was in spite of his lack of an official position, something that otherwise mattered enormously in the educational hierarchies of Austria-Hungary and Germany. In November he began giving a course of lectures on aesthetics and composition at the Stern Conservatoire; while they elicited little response among the general public, they were much appreciated by his friends and admirers among the intellectuals and visual artists.

As Schoenberg had hoped, he experienced a burst of creative energy. During the summer of 1911 he had finished his book on harmony and had returned to the orchestration of *Gurrelieder*, finally completing the score in Berlin. Biographical accounts of this period vary in their assessment of Schoenberg's state of mind. Berlin, it seems, offered Schoenberg more space, freedom and opportunities to meet artists who were interested in his music and ideas, and he was now finally able to meet Busoni in person. It is not hard to see how, through his contacts with the writer Alfred Döblin, the painter Emil Nolde and Herwarth Walden, he must have sensed that the isolation which was a part of his Viennese existence was being replaced in Berlin by a dynamic flow of new ideas around him. The publication of Kandinsky's *Über das Geistige in der Kunst* ('On the Spiritual in Art') at Christmas 1911 would have been of great interest to him, since it offered a rationale for non-representational art. Schoenberg's resentment towards Vienna became a recurrent theme in his letters, and when the Music Academy there offered him a teaching post he declined it. Nevertheless, periods of self-doubt continued and at one point he wrote to Berg:

I've lost all interest in my work. I'm not satisfied with anything anymore. I see mistakes and inadequacies in everything. Enough of that; I can't begin to tell you how I feel at such times. It's not ambition. Otherwise, I would be satisfied that there are some people who think better of it than I do.

A creative challenge presented itself in late January 1912 when the actress Albertine Zehme asked Schoenberg to write the music for her recitations of Otto Erich Hartleben's German version of poems from Albert Giraud's collection *Pierrot lunaire* ('The Moonstruck Pierrot'). The poetry was not new to Schoenberg: in 1904 Max Marschalk's settings from *Pierrot* had been performed during one of the concerts of the Ansorge Society, and by 1912 several other settings existed. Zehme had declaimed the verse to the accompaniment of some music by Otto Vriesländer, but she was not satisfied and was looking for something more original.

Schoenberg's *Pierrot lunaire* – or to give its full title, *Dreimal sieben Gedichte aus Albert Girauds Pierrot lunaire* ('Three Times Seven Poems from Albert Giraud's *Pierrot lunaire*') – is now considered one of the high points (Stravinsky called it 'the solar plexus') of European Modernism. Schoenberg believed in the mystical significance of numbers and so selected 21 poems, stressing the basic unit of seven, which is of major importance in this system. He was also aware that the number of poems would be the same as the work's opus number.

Zehme's part was notated – but in a particular way, for Schoenberg indicated only the approximate pitches and required the performer to chant the text somewhere between song and speech. As this manner of performance, called *Sprechgesang* ('intoned speech'), cannot be precisely determined, it results in a variety of individual performances. Schoenberg had done something similar in the *Gurrelieder* but in a manner that was closer to traditional melodrama, with the performer speaking against the background of music (as in Beethoven's *Fidelio*, Weber's and Marschner's operas, and, closer to Schoenberg's time, Richard Strauss's and Engelbert Humperdinck's attempts to revive this style). In *Pierrot* the poetry was to be given fluid inflexions, akin to the cabaret style of delivery with which Schoenberg was familiar.

Hartleben's *Pierrot* is a *commedia dell'arte* character: sarcastic and sadistic, he is at the mercy of the moon, surrounded by symbols, and hiding behind a mask. He and his world are much more sinister than Stravinsky's Petrushka, the other contemporary half-man/half-puppet, and this quality is emphasized by Schoenberg's music. The instrumental ensemble does more than accompany the voice: it carries the essence of the composition and creates the drama. Each song develops its own complex form (often based on the contrapuntal

devices of canon and fugue), and the labyrinth of free-flowing musical ideas present in *Erwartung* and *Die glückliche Hand* has been
replaced by formal tautness and an order that creates vibrant immediacy. The intoned vocal line is not accompanied in a traditional
sense; rather, the main musical content of the piece is presented by
an ensemble of five players who between them perform on eight different instruments. It is as if the melodic lines of the instruments,
with their constantly changing timbres, realize the full musical potential which the expressive semi-speech cannot achieve on its own.

Schoenberg and Albertine
Zehme with the members of
the instrumental ensemble
after the first performance
of *Pierrot lunaire*, Berlin,
16 October 1912 (left to
right): Karl Essberger, Jakob
Maliniak, Schoenberg,
Albertine Zehme, Eduard
Steuermann, Hans Kindler
and Hans de Vries.

Before *Pierrot lunaire* could be presented to the public on
16 October 1912, many rehearsals were needed to bring together the
tricky speaking part, the virtuoso lines of the individual instruments,
and the complex dynamic shadings. The success of the première
meant that Zehme's original plan to take the work on a tour of
Germany and Austria could now be put into practice without reser-
vation. Some fifteen performances followed before the end of the

Schoenberg with his pupils
and friends in Berlin, 1912
(left to right): Paul Königer,
Edward Clark, Erwin Stein,
Eduard Steuermann,
Schoenberg, Hans Nachod,
Heinrich Jalowetz, Anton
Webern and Josef Polnauer.

year, most of them conducted by Schoenberg – although Hermann
Scherchen took over during November when Schoenberg had to
conduct *Pelleas und Melisande* in Amsterdam. In December,
Stravinsky heard *Pierrot* in Berlin and later recorded his unease
with the poetry, which he considered to be 'a retrogression to the
out-of-date Beardsley cult'. Stravinsky's rather detached view of
the poetry alone suggests that he had failed to appreciate the extent
to which Hartleben's versions of Giraud's poetry made it much
more open to Schoenberg's Modernist interpretation.

    It soon became clear that Zehme fell short of Schoenberg's
expectations and disappointed those who, like Scherchen, had

understood the work's full musical and theatrical significance; however, she held the performing rights and was convinced of her worth. She later tried to manoeuvre Schoenberg into engaging her as a reciter in the *Gurrelieder*, promising financial help from her wealthy husband. Although Zehme had a volatile character and could explode into dramatic rage, her link with Schoenberg continued, and at one time she even put her villa in Berlin at the disposal of his family. Only after World War I did Erika Wagner and Marya Freund emerge as the performers who were capable of doing the work full justice.

 Pierrot certainly brought about a considerable change in Schoenberg's daily life. In both Vienna and Berlin he had normally been preoccupied with teaching, while, apart from the regular summer breaks, he had travelled very little. Now he had to make time in order to tour Germany with *Pierrot* and conduct *Pelleas* abroad. The Amsterdam and The Hague performances of *Pelleas* in November 1912 were well received and the following engagement took him to St Petersburg in December. The conductor and pianist Alexander Siloti had included *Pelleas* in one of his orchestral concerts but, rather than conducting the work himself, invited Schoenberg as a guest conductor. Here he found himself the centre of attention, and he was impressed both by the standard of the orchestra and by the seriousness with which his music was approached.

 Schoenberg was now conscious that he was appreciated abroad rather more than in Germany, let alone in Vienna. It was not just the hostility in Vienna that had caused his earlier problems; usually several years had to pass before a work of Schoenberg's lost its aura of difficulty and strangeness, and concert directors and conductors could cope with it. Interestingly, it was Sir Henry Wood in London who included the as yet unperformed Five Orchestral Pieces in a Promenade Concert on 3 September 1912. The London public's earlier encounter with Schoenberg's music, when Richard Buhlig performed the Piano Pieces, Op. 11, on 23 January that year, had met with the usual hostility from the press. *The Times* had reported that in the Piano Pieces 'there was hardly a bar which did not sound affected and certainly not one which was not ugly. It only made one regret that Mr Buhlig should be wasting his fine and delicate talent over it.' On 4 September, however, the tone was different and *The Times*'s critic gave the Orchestral Pieces the benefit of the doubt: 'Whether [the music] has a real message it is simply too early to say. At the conclusion half the audience hissed. That seems a too decisive judgement, for after all they may turn out to be wrong.' This was, at least, a fair attempt by a less than enthusiastic reviewer to come to grips with the idiom while avoiding the high-handed dismissiveness which would persist among conservative London critics even as late as the 1940s.

Once the orchestration of the *Gurrelieder* was completed in June 1912, months of strenuous work were needed to produce a serviceable piano reduction of the gargantuan score – which Berg undertook to prepare. Despite Schoenberg's declaration that he did not want any new work of his to have its première in Vienna, he realized that Franz Schreker's willingness to rehearse the demanding work was an opportunity not to be missed. An important aspect of Schoenberg's determination to complete a work that he had begun in an earlier style was his desire to dispel the malicious claim that his recent music was cast in an advanced dissonant idiom because he lacked the traditional composing skills. The première of the oratorio – in Vienna in February 1913 – was received with great enthusiasm, but this did not signal a tectonic change in the general attitude towards Schoenberg, and only five weeks later a concert at which, in addition to his Chamber Symphony and works by Zemlinsky and Mahler, he conducted his pupils' works, was greeted with the familiar, disruptive noise. Kraus once again came to Schoenberg's defence and *Die Fackel* carried a strong condemnation of the new depths to which the Viennese press had sunk.

The *Gurrelieder*, although stylistically still part of the late nineteenth century, had its disturbing innovative moments. The lyricism of its first part gave way to a powerful representation of Waldemar's men being condemned to a never-ending nocturnal hunt. The melodrama of the narrator, the monologue of Klaus the Fool and the orchestral apotheosis mixed the grandiloquent with the sarcastic, indicating the uneasy coexistence of the heroic and self-destructive tendencies in the human psyche. Thus, the decade in which Freud and the Expressionists had presented their ideas – and the one in which Mahler's music had become better known – enabled the *Gurrelieder* to be better understood. The close proximity of such different works as the *Gurrelieder*, *Die glückliche Hand* and

Pierrot well illustrates the discontinuities of Modernism. Waldemar
is forever left to the mercy of forces he cannot control; Pierrot's world
is controlled by the alien and sinister light of the moon; and the
macabre violence to which he subjects Cassander exposes the dark
undercurrent that is concealed by the expressionless surface of a
masked, clown-like figure. In the first scene of *Die glückliche Hand*,
a fantastic beast of the unconscious sits on the Man's back, making
the rest of the work appear as a gruesome nightmare. When one
considers that the musical argument of each of these works was
conceived in a thoroughly different way, it could be argued that this
period of Schoenberg's life involved one of the most significant bursts
of creative energy ever to have been experienced by a composer.

Kandinsky had warned Schoenberg that concert performances
would sap his time and creative energy, and in 1914 his compositional

activity did indeed seem to be slackening. In January 1914 he was
in London to conduct a new performance of the Five Orchestral
Pieces, Op. 16, while in March he conducted the first German
performance of the *Gurrelieder* in Leipzig and, only two weeks later,
Pierrot in Regensberg. Irrespective of professional engagements,
however, it would have been difficult for Schoenberg to sustain the
earlier flow of creativity. Nevertheless, at the end of 1913 there came
a setting of Stefan George's translation of Ernest Dowson's sonnet
Seraphita. This was the first set of the Four Orchestral Songs comprising Op. 22; the other three songs, settings of poems by Rainer
Maria Rilke, would be added a year or so later. The sketch of a
theme for the orchestral scherzo of a projected symphony is of
historical importance only because it contained all twelve notes
of the chromatic scale stated only once; it therefore heralds
Schoenberg's twelve-note method of composition, which properly
belongs to the years after World War I.

   With hindsight it might be said that the frenetic artistic activity
throughout Europe and the seemingly insatiable desire to break out
of all traditional moulds were symptoms of tension and foreboding –
a tacit realization that imperialist aspirations threatened to start a
conflagration, which artists attempted to counter by asserting the
dominance of the creative spirit over the irrationality of politics.
But the irrationality that is encountered as a theme and method in
so much of the artistic activity was not a passive reflection of political tensions. Rather, it was as if artists were capturing the spectre
of things to come as a warning whose full significance even they
could not grasp.

5

A self-conscious soldier:
Schoenberg in uniform, 1916.

All that was stirring within him still lay in darkness, and yet he already felt the desire to gaze into this darkness, with all the shapes that populated it, which the others did not notice. There was a thin prickling chill mingled with this desire. It was as though over his life there would now always be nothing but a grey, veiled sky – great clouds, monstrous changing forms, and the ever-renewed question: Are they monsters? Are they merely clouds?

Robert Musil,
Die Verwirrungen des Zöglings Törless
('The Confusions of Young Törless')

The Last Days of Kakania 1914-19

There was nothing particular that distinguished the early summer of 1914 – in Vienna, Berlin and elsewhere it was as ever a period when musical activity wound down and composers could contemplate a period of undisturbed work in some rural idyll. That year Kandinsky offered to find Schoenberg a house in the Bavarian village of Murnau where he now lived, and in June Schoenberg replied: 'I intend to spend the holidays in Bavaria – that is from 4 July to 13/14 August. And since I would like to compose a lot, I must live very peacefully and undisturbed.' The spring and early summer had been filled with engagements and plans for future performances. Alexander Siloti was keen to have *Pierrot* performed in St Petersburg but Schoenberg resisted the idea, fearing that the performers there would not be ready for another year or two (unbeknown to him, Siloti's wife was trying to overcome this resistance by approaching Zehme directly). Schoenberg's sketch in May of the scherzo fragment with a twelve-note theme was a good indication that compositional tasks pressed heavily and that everything else would be a distraction. It was as if the characters in a tragedy were living in a state of delusion while the gods plotted disaster.

The assassination of Archduke Franz Ferdinand in Sarajevo on 28 June 1914 at first looked as if it would turn into just another typically Balkan crisis, but by the beginning of August it was threatening to turn into a war involving most European nations through various alliances. German and Austrian intellectuals reacted to its outbreak with surprising acquiescence, and even the writer Gerhart Hauptmann and the theatrical director Max Reinhardt signed the manifesto of ninety-three German intellectuals who supported the war aims. In *Gedanken im Kriege* ('Thoughts in Wartime'), published in *Die Neue Rundschau* in November 1914, Thomas Mann described the war as a 'purification', a 'liberation' and an 'immense hope'. Schoenberg did not feel any different at first and in the early stages of the war expressed himself several times in favour of the German and

Austrian struggle against 'the barbarians'. While a loyalty to the Emperor was to sustain Schoenberg throughout the war, Berg became sceptical, and Kraus, with whom Schoenberg remained in touch throughout the hostilities, gradually emerged as one of the war's most eloquent critics.

The saying that the Muses are silent in times of war was only superficially true in Schoenberg's case. Admittedly, his compositional activity slowed down and whatever hopes he might have had for the summer of 1914 were dampened as a new sense of insecurity made itself felt. By January 1915 he had finished only three of the Four Orchestral Songs, Op. 22 (the fourth followed in 1916). Nevertheless his loss of a stable social environment led him to conceive the text for a large oratorio, *Die Jakobsleiter* ('Jacob's Ladder'). The text explored the nature of belief, existence and the human relationship with God, and the ambitious philosophical scheme was to be given a commensurate musical interpretation. The oratorio would be one of his most problematic works, together with the opera *Moses und Aron*, and would remain unfinished as though in tragic confirmation of the enormousness of the intellectual task that Schoenberg had set himself.

When Alma Mahler visited the composer in Berlin in January 1915, she found him as intellectually alert as ever, and admired the skill with which he made furniture and decorated his family's apartment. But Schoenberg's financial insecurity had worsened as life in wartime Berlin became more and more difficult. Alma had the idea that Schoenberg should come to Vienna to conduct a performance of Beethoven's Ninth Symphony, which would include Mahler's retouches to the orchestration; the financial guarantor was going to be her wealthy friend Lilly Lieser. The performance, on 26 April 1915, was far from a success, however. Schoenberg did not get on with the orchestra during the rehearsals, and this was reflected in a performance that so embarrassed Alma that she hid from Schoenberg after the concert, while a few devoted friends, including Berg and Eduard Steuermann (who had become Schoenberg's pupil and collaborator in 1912), tried to save the situation by applauding loudly. Schnitzler recorded in his diary only that Schoenberg 'directed in a boring manner', and the newspaper *Ostdeutsche Rundschau* slated Schoenberg, adding anti-Semitic asides and, as usual, bewailing the besmirching of German culture: 'He did not betray even a trace of an attempt at a conception that would strive after the work's content, let alone of penetration into the lofty spirit of this eternal monument to Germany's cultural greatness.'

In May, Italy entered the war on the side of the Triple Entente (Britain, France and Russia), and Austria had to open another front. Call-ups intensified, Berg started military service in May, and Schoenberg, having been rejected earlier on medical grounds (he was a lifelong sufferer from asthma), was now pronounced fit for service although he was not called up until November. The arcane rules of Austro-Hungarian bureaucracy deemed Schoenberg, because of his

Zemlinsky (seated) and Schoenberg in Prague, c. 1917. Zemlinsky had moved to Prague in 1911 and remained there until 1927.

father's birthplace, a Hungarian citizen and therefore under the jurisdiction of the Defence Ministry in Budapest. His friends, as well as
the Tonkünstlerverein, tried to get him released from service or at
least transferred to the jurisdiction of Vienna, and even sought the
Hungarian composer Béla Bartók's help in the matter. But Schoenberg
found an easier solution and joined as a one-year volunteer. This gave
him the right to choose a regiment, and he opted for the long-established Hoch- und Deutschmeister Regiment, usually commanded by
a member of the House of Habsburg. Three weeks before joining the
army, Schoenberg wrote a will – a prudent yet desperate act arising
from the inevitable foreboding before military service.

As Schoenberg's preoccupations at the time involved questions
of identity, existence and the meaning of life, it is significant that he
started work on the *Jakobsleiter* in January 1915, when the war began
to go wrong for Austria. Russia managed to reverse her early defeat
and captured the fortress of Przemyśl in March 1915, and it may well
be that the gathering gloom had contributed to the débâcle when
Schoenberg conducted Beethoven's Ninth. Schoenberg's increased
introspection – together with a fatalistic search for omens, widespread
at the time – is reflected in his resuming the writing of a diary,
soon after the war broke out. He had begun a diary in Berlin in
January 1912, but kept it going only for a few months. This earlier
diary is interesting because it recorded his feelings towards the
Berlin musicians and revealed a sense of vulnerability combined
with a determined belief in his own creative power. The new diary
was very different, for it consisted entirely of careful day-by-day
descriptions of the shape, direction and colour of the clouds, reading
them as indicators of future events:

> *September 24: about 10:45 a.m.:*
> *icy-cold mood, <u>like in a circus before a very daring stunt</u>: silence,*
> *tension, no wind; impression of the sky is at first predominantly*
> *clear, pure; only later I observe a slowly expanding cloud streak.*
> *Total impression: a daring operation which began under*
> *auspicious circumstances.*

It is as if the anthropomorphism of Expressionist writers was taken
by Schoenberg as a reliable means of linking his inner self with the

surrounding world. Together with many early twentieth-century
Modernists, Schoenberg was drawn towards the arcane, and his
fascination with portents, astrology and numerology was shared by
many of his pupils. Like Schoenberg, Berg was particularly plagued
by the number 13, and his Chamber Concerto (1925) is a monument
to the numerological fascination shared by Schoenberg and those
around him.

It may be difficult to accept that an obsession with numbers has
anything to do with the scientific positivism of the early years of the
twentieth century. Yet if, as the nineteenth-century philosopher and
physicist Ernst Mach argued, mental phenomena can be reduced
to physical facts, then those who are less troubled with rigorous scientific proof can readily accept that numbers are the most logical
links between the inner self and the outside world. The numero-
logical fascination was only one aspect of the search for the meaning
of life, and other fashionable trends included Emanuel Swedenborg's
mysticism and Rudolf Steiner's anthroposophy. All these ideas
exercised Schoenberg and his circle, and were intensified by the
uncertainty caused by the war.

Schoenberg's health had never been strong and the discomfort of
military life could not have been easy to bear, particularly as he was
forty years old when the war started. Between March and May 1916
he attended an officers' training school in Bruck-an-der-Leitha, east
of Vienna, only a few miles away from Haydn's birthplace, Rohrau.
Schoenberg's age had saved him from front-line service and he performed his duties enthusiastically. He also worked on several march
settings, but completed only one, *Die eiserne Brigade* ('The Iron
Brigade'), for string quartet and piano, intended for a social evening.
By May, Schoenberg was back in Vienna, his asthma aggravated
by the unpleasant climate in Bruck-an-der-Leitha. This facilitated
his transfer to lighter duties in a reserve battalion, followed by temporary discharge.

The old imperial Austria, towards which Schoenberg felt that
particular loyalty which frequently united people of disparate
political beliefs and cultural sensibilities, was slowly disintegrating.
No longer the preserve of Balkan hotheads, political assassination
became a reality in Vienna too when, in October 1916, Friedrich
Adler, son of the Socialist Democratic leader Victor Adler,

Schoenberg (front row, second from right) at the reserve officers' school, Bruck-an-der-Leitha, 1916.

assassinated Count Stürgkh, the head of the Reichsrat. A month later came the death of the aged Franz Josef – to some the benign head of a large family of nations, to others an ossified irrelevance. He was succeeded by his great-nephew Karl, who was never crowned Emperor and would preside over the dissolution of the monarchy two years later.

The gloomy atmosphere in Vienna and the weakness of the Austrian position in the war affected Schoenberg deeply and he wrote to Karl Kraus about the spiritual crisis in which he found himself. When Schoenberg was discharged in October 1916, he did not return to composition with the same intensity that had characterized the pre-war years. His main project was the text for *Die Jakobsleiter*, which he completed in May 1917. Although he started composing the oratorio almost immediately, matters of everyday existence loomed even larger than this grandiose work. He was called up again and spent the autumn and early winter of 1917 in a music battalion in Vienna. Eugenie Schwarzwald came to his aid once more, first by trying to organize financial help, and then, at about the same time

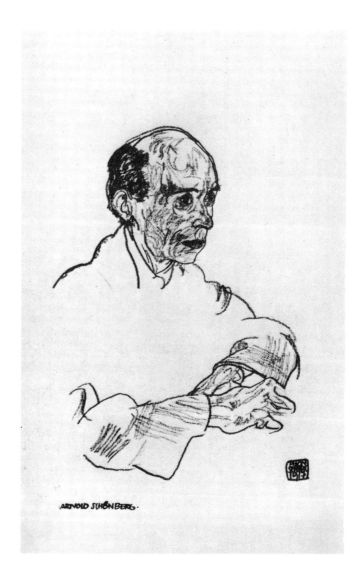

Schoenberg, drawing by
Egon Schiele, 1917. The
image is disturbingly
prescient and reveals
Schoenberg as he would
look in the 1940s.

as he had to report for army duty, by offering him another opportunity to hold composition courses in her school. This second period
of military service was a perfunctory affair, and Schoenberg started
his course at the Schwarzwald-Schule only a few days after reporting
for duty on 19 September 1917. Then the question of accommodation
for his family arose, as it frequently did – one of the many crises that

plagued the family's existence in Vienna. The goodwill of Frau
Lieser, Alma Mahler's friend who had offered the Schoenbergs
lodgings on their return from Berlin, seemed to have run out,
tensions arose, and in October the family had to live for a while in
a cheap boarding house. They managed to move for a couple of
months to a flat in the Rechte Bahngasse, their last address in
Vienna, and in spring 1918, Schoenberg having been demobilized the
previous December, they settled in Mödling, near Vienna. The rent
of their Mödling house (now a Schoenberg museum) was paid by
Schoenberg's cousin and foster-sister Olga Nachod, now Baroness
Pascotini, whose wealth derived not from her adventurer husband but
from a devoted lover who was a rich Viennese industrialist. There is
a touch of fantasy here, as in a novel – the reappearance of a relative
who was repaying the kindness that the Schoenbergs had shown
her as an orphan. But this was no happy ending – just a brief respite
during a very traumatic time.

The army leaders, who had persuaded Franz Josef that it would
be a good thing to teach Serbia a lesson for its alleged implications in
the assassination of the Emperor's nephew, were not just unaware of
what they were starting, they also seriously misunderstood the nature
of modern warfare, and it soon turned out that Austrian industrial
resources were unable to sustain the war effort. There had been a
brief wave of hope after the Austrian victory in October 1917 on the
Italian front at Caporetto (now Kobarid, in Slovenia), but the frag-
mented nature of the Austro-Hungarian Dual Monarchy meant that
the war could continue only with extensive aid brought about by a
German-dictated economic union. In January 1918 flour rations in
Austria were reduced from 200 to 165 grams per person per day and
strikes began, first in Vienna but soon as far afield as Hungary.
Ominous signs that the Dual Monarchy was unlikely to survive,
whatever the outcome of the war, were becoming more numerous.
Early in 1918 the left wing of the Social Democrats under Otto Bauer
distanced itself from the Greater Austrian programme advocated by
Karl Renner, and Czech leaders simultaneously proclaimed that the
Czech and Slovak nations were freeing themselves from the monarchy.

As the times were not conducive to creative work, Schoenberg
devoted himself to teaching. This also meant that he had to think
intensely about theoretical principles. His seeming lack of inspiration

and the difficulty of progressing with the *Jakobsleiter* were actually indicators of a crisis which, instead of inhibiting activity altogether, made him contemplate the links between technical issues and questions about the nature of imagination and intuition. This further led to the need to formulate compositional principles that would not reflect passing stylistic fashions but reach, as it were, into the very essence of musicality as he saw it. That such efforts were linked with a search for spiritual fulfilment is only one more sign that Schoenberg's musical language was not 'dry' and 'cerebral', as his detractors would later claim. Admittedly, he was facing a difficulty. His desire to achieve a close union between a clear, logical musical procedure and a super-sensual, mystic revelation to which the musical 'idea' or 'thought' would lead required his wider audience to rise to an ambitious level of perception and introspection.

At the close of the sixteenth century, Renaissance artists had been deliberately searching for a quality of 'difficulty', believing that the effort needed to surmount it gave rise to virtue. Schoenberg's attitude had a distant affinity with this – especially where it concerned the synthesis of the aesthetic and the ethical. Those closest to Schoenberg, especially Berg and Webern, were also inspired to look for this unity, and each of them produced his own version. Berg's was moving slowly towards its full realization via the interaction of his numero-logical belief with the psycho-sociological components of his two operas. Webern, who shared with Schoenberg a fascination for Goethe's pantheistic belief in the omnipresence of ideal forms, pursued his version of unity by means of an obsessive attention to structural details and the refinement of expression. Others in Schoenberg's circle, though weaker as creative personalities, were aware of being exposed to the influence of a man possessing an original musical mind that they could not find in anyone else. Conversely, Schoenberg increasingly believed that his only hope was to address his music to those willing to invest the required effort.

As military crises and political tensions worsened, those around Schoenberg formed a tighter, alternative community that was guided not by the irrationality of war and politics, but by the devotion to a moral and aesthetic ideal. As prime and foreign ministers came and went (and as one of the foreign ministers, Stephan von Burián, even mooted the possibility of informal peace talks with the Entente),

Schoenberg's *Die Jakobsleiter*, a page of the short score, 1917. Schoenberg worked on the oratorio between 1917 and 1922 and again briefly in 1944, but never completed it.

Schoenberg began talking to Berg and Webern about a forum for the performance of new music. This occurred at a time when their unity of purpose was being torn apart from within, since the crises in society only exacerbated the personal tensions that were never far from Schoenberg and his circle; even seemingly small disagreements tended to explode into profound crises. At one point Webern, then a frequent visitor to Mödling, announced his intention of moving back to Prague in search of work. This was enough to bring charges

of treason from Schoenberg and it took several months before their
differences were patched up. After their reconciliation, preparations
for the formation of a Verein für private Musikaufführungen (Society
for Private Musical Performances) were well under way. The Society
was formally inaugurated on 23 November 1918, less than two weeks
after the abdications of the German Kaiser and the Austro-Hungarian
Emperor. On the day after the Emperor's abdication, the provisional
parliament in Vienna proclaimed the Republic of Deutsch-Österreich
(Germany-Austria). The Czecho-Slovak Republic, the Hungarian
Republic, and the State of the Serbs, Croats and Slovenes – the future
Yugoslavia – had already been proclaimed. The old Kakania, as
Musil irreverently called it, had disappeared. But, by creating a forum
in which to uphold their artistic integrity, Schoenberg and his
associates must have felt that they were compensating for the collapse
of the social order around them with an act of personal defiance.

6

A pensive Schoenberg in the
early 1920s.

I sought beauty. To it I sacrificed everything:
no aim was sacrosanct, no means clear-cut.
Unrestrained, I stormed to the goal; untested,
I stifled my natural disposition; unhesitating,
I subordinated all meaning to form.

Arnold Schoenberg,
Die Jakobsleiter

Searching for Truth in Vienna 1919–25

The belief in the efficiency of the Austro-Hungarian administration was widespread before and after its demise. It is touching, amusing even, to see how the founders of the Society for Private Musical Performances relied on that bureaucratic model. The Society's statutes, drafted under Schoenberg's supervision, contained intricate rules and assigned hierarchical positions to various members of its governing body. Hans Keller later construed this as a closed society which was creating a circumscribed ideological world, but the reality was, perhaps, more complex. Undoubtedly, the vanishing state was, as far as Schoenberg's private world was concerned, to be replaced by a Society that was united by an artistic purpose. He and his colleagues reflected the belief, widespread in Vienna, that exposure to culture could substitute for the past glory of the Empire. However nostalgic he might have felt, Schoenberg also knew that the Society needed a European dimension if it were to have substance, and in this spirit he wrote, in a memorandum to the Society's members, that they 'may like to consider that in these sad times, when everything in Austria is collapsing, our Society is the one event with a European orientation'. This internationalism was yet another of the many contradictions in Schoenberg's actions and beliefs; although his wartime patriotism had become tinged with a dislike of enemy intellectuals and musicians, the Society's first concert featured works by Debussy, whom Schoenberg had previously criticized for his anti-German stance, and the Russian Alexander Scriabin, against whose country Austria had fought with particular bitterness.

Schoenberg believed that the audience's lack of understanding of his music (and that of his circle) was due primarily to poorly prepared performances, and that the negative reception given to his concerts was conditioned by the critics' hostility and prejudice. He hoped that the Society would deal with the first problem by offering several open rehearsals of each piece, thus involving the audience in a learning process. As for the second problem, critics were not to be especially

invited, although they could pay their fee and become members
of the Society. Consequently, applause and other audible signs of
(dis)approval were not allowed. Schoenberg shaped the Society as he
wanted it to be and the rumour was put about that he was simply
creating a forum for his own music. In fact he avoided performing his
own works while generously including works by contemporaries, such
as Debussy and Strauss, for whom he otherwise did not have much
sympathy. Aesthetic differences between Schoenberg and Stravinsky
were not yet in evidence, and in April 1919 he asked the Russian composer for a new work, promptly receiving from him the score of the
Three Pieces for String Quartet. In the event, it was not the Quartet
but Stravinsky's *Trois Pièces faciles* and *Cinq Pièces faciles* that were
performed, followed in June by his *Pribaoutki* and the *Berceuse du
chat*, with Schoenberg himself taking charge of the rehearsals.

As the Society could afford to engage only a small number of performers its repertoire was limited to chamber music, and orchestral
compositions were presented in ingenious chamber-music adaptations.
This resulted in little masterpieces such as the arrangements of
Mahler's *Das Lied von der Erde* and *Lieder eines fahrenden Gesellen*
by Schoenberg and Erwin Stein, Debussy's *Prélude à l'après-midi
d'un faune* by Benno Sachs, and waltzes by members of the Viennese
Strauss family arranged by Schoenberg, Berg and Webern. But the
times were not auspicious for the Society's survival. Funds were lacking
and the Society was kept alive only by considerable self-sacrifice on
the part of Schoenberg's friends and the performers who were offered
meagre fees. The diminished post-war Austria was experiencing a
lingering economic crisis and inflation, though less extreme than that
which raged in Germany during the early years of the Weimar
Republic. In September 1921 the Society would have to be wound up,
and its activity transferred to its Prague branch headed by Zemlinsky.

For income over this period Schoenberg had to rely solely on the
fees from the courses he gave at the Schwarzwald-Schule, although
his finances improved as a result of conducting engagements in
Germany and the Netherlands and the royalties from performances
of the *Gurrelieder*. Dutch musicians, especially the conductor Willem
Mengelberg, were particularly interested in Schoenberg, and soon
after his second visit to Amsterdam, in May 1920, when he attended
the Mahler festival organized by Mengelberg, he was invited to

return there for a season and combine teaching and conducting. Fortunately, his Schwarzwald-Schule courses had recently attracted several extremely talented students and he was able to take on two of them, Max Deutsch and Hanns Eisler, as his teaching assistants. At the end of September he and his family rented a house at Zandvoort, where he taught and from where he frequently travelled to Amsterdam to rehearse with the Concertgebouw Orchestra. But the combination of teaching and commuting turned out to be too demanding, and before long he was complaining that he had no time left for composition. Moreover, he was happy to be able to work with a renowned orchestra, but was also aware that his 'autocratic make-up', as he himself characterized it, did not go down well in the civilized, calm atmosphere that prevailed in the Concertgebouw, and by March 1921 he was back in Vienna.

Alma Mahler (seated) with Schoenberg on her left, surrounded by participants at the Mahler festival in Amsterdam, May 1920.

The first initiatives of the Society for Private Musical Performances coincided with an emerging awareness among publishers and the younger critics that new music mattered. In Vienna, Universal Edition founded a periodical, *Musikblätter des Anbruch*, which was devoted to contemporary topics and which soon became an influential publication. Schoenberg felt slighted not to have been mentioned in the first issue of November 1919 – and this became a source of grievance towards the otherwise consistently Modernist journal (which the young philosopher and composer Theodor Wiesengrund, later Adorno, edited in the late 1920s). In Germany the newly founded *Melos* was edited by Hermann Scherchen, Schoenberg's student and close collaborator who, as well as making a name for himself as a conductor, had become prominent in the Independent German Socialist Party's cultural branch. *Melos* was much more supportive of Schoenberg, although a mixture of political intrigue and financial problems soon caused Scherchen to step down. In January 1920 the Viennese publisher E. P. Tal wanted to commission a book on Schoenberg and asked the composer to suggest an author. Schoenberg's first choice was Berg, but his former pupil, forever torn between his family affairs and the preparation of Schoenberg's scores for publication, declined and the book was written by the maverick Egon Wellesz. Wellesz's early distance from Schoenberg's inner circle was viewed as an impediment, although when the book came out in 1921 Schoenberg admitted to Berg that it was 'surprisingly good'. Its English translation followed immediately and for a long time it remained the standard book on Schoenberg's early period in the English-speaking world.

By the end of the war Schoenberg was still relatively unknown in France. While one might think that his wartime partisan stance would count against him, surprisingly the reverse was the case and the leading French Modernists – the older Maurice Ravel and the younger Francis Poulenc, Darius Milhaud and Arthur Honegger – began to show a keen interest in his music. Ravel, who visited Vienna in October 1920 at the time that Schoenberg was in Zandvoort, had distanced himself during the war from chauvinistic outbursts by his French colleagues, and in this respect he proved to be more broad-minded than Schoenberg had been. Erwin Stein remembers that Ravel came up with some superlatives about Schoenberg's piano music, although, if Alma Mahler is to be believed, his reaction varied, depending on the work. She recalls Ravel saying that Schoenberg's Chamber Symphony was not music but something that had come 'out of a laboratory'. Poulenc and Milhaud first came in direct contact with Schoenberg in January 1922, when two performances of *Pierrot lunaire* with different soloists, reciting in French and German, were conducted by Milhaud and Schoenberg respectively. The psychological tensions of Schoenberg's cycle that were concealed beneath the mask of the *commedia dell'arte* characters must have resonated with Milhaud's own desire to stress the absurd, even if the violence in the scenario of his ballet *Le Boeuf sur le toit* ('The Bull on the Roof') was somewhat neutralized by his collaborator Jean Cocteau's whimsical treatment of it. Schoenberg hugely enjoyed a four-hand version of *Le Boeuf* which Poulenc and Milhaud played to him and he subsequently singled out Milhaud as a significant innovator in the music of the 'Latin nations'.

Schoenberg's later ridiculing of Stravinsky, whose move to a neo-Bachian aesthetic he found baffling after the earlier, more Modernist works, has inspired the belief that Schoenberg was innately opposed to all aspects of neo-classicism. But it is truer to say that he was critical of the tendency to opt for a 'serious' pastiche of past styles, while Poulenc's and Milhaud's lighter touch, together with their preference for witty parody, appealed to him. Indeed, he retained a high regard for Milhaud to the end of his life, even if a small cloud appeared on the horizon during the time that they both lived in California. While praising Milhaud in a conversation, Schoenberg also remarked that he composed 'too much' and an indiscreet mutual friend reported this to Milhaud, who took it badly.

The distrust between Schoenberg and Stravinsky – who had moved to France in 1920 – was not, at first, very pronounced. Of course, Stravinsky's early misgivings about *Pierrot* indicated his difficulty in relating to Schoenberg's aesthetic sphere, of which the music was but a part; nevertheless, their first post-war contacts were encouraging. There is even a Stravinskian allusion – a distinct recurring phrase dominated by the clarinet – in the 'Tanzszene' of Schoenberg's Serenade, Op. 24, possibly dating from the time when Stravinsky was being performed by the Society. By about 1923 the teacher Nadia Boulanger was analysing Schoenberg with her students in Paris,

Igor Stravinsky, c. 1920.
Schoenberg showed an
interest in Stravinsky's music
immediately after World
War I, but by 1924 had
become very critical
of Stravinsky's version
of neo-classicism.

although this was not for long: she had become increasingly drawn
to the influential xenophobic group known as *Action Française*, but
may also have succumbed to pressure from Stravinsky not to give
prominence to Schoenberg's music in her classes.

The political polarization of the immediate post-war years was
an inevitable reaction to the real or imagined danger of social revo-
lution. Austria escaped revolutionary violence, but it happened on
her doorstep in 1919 – during the short-lived Soviet Republic in
Munich, and during the regime of Béla Kun in Hungary. Austrian
politics reacted to these upheavals as if they were a present danger
at home. A number of paramilitary groups sprang up, especially in
the border areas of Salzburg and Carinthia; these were eventually
organized into the *Heimwehren*, right-wing militias, and supported
financially by their Bavarian counterparts. Anti-Semitism became
one of the banners under which these groups were united, and the
Austrian right-wingers were also convinced that the provinces were
suffering because of the pernicious influence of Vienna, where the
Social Democrats were strong. The tension between the oversized
capital of the new, reduced Austria and the conservative Catholic
countryside created a serious political problem.

Schoenberg experienced this in a particularly unpleasant form when, in June 1921, in an optimistic frame of mind and with plans to complete the *Jakobsleiter* and revise the *Harmonielehre*, he went on holiday with his family and friends to the Mattsee near Salzburg. Felix Greissle (soon to be Schoenberg's son-in-law) initially reported to Berg that Schoenberg was working well, but before long posters had appeared in Mattsee declaring that Jews were not welcome. This was followed by an official written request that Schoenberg's party should leave. Having considered himself a Christian for years, Schoenberg was shattered. The Viennese press, commenting on the incident, wondered whether the federal Austrian laws were indeed in force in Salzburg, but a Salzburg paper almost accused Schoenberg of having staged it all. The whole incident was played down with the explanation that there had been anti-Jewish feeling in the area since the wartime presence there of Jewish refugees from Galicia. But Schoenberg's perception of the incident was sharper, more pessimistic and, in the long run, tragically true. He realized that the new rabble-rousers now had fertile ground for the dissemination of anti-Jewish hatred, something that had always lurked beneath the surface of national and religious tolerance in the old Austria-Hungary. It is therefore not surprising that Schoenberg not only started to reflect on his Jewish identity but also became nostalgically attached to the memory of the House of Habsburg. However, he was far removed from the monarchist sentiments, mixed with xenophobia, that some of the Christian Socialists adhered to; he was motivated by a yearning for the religious tolerance of which Franz Josef had been seen as the guarantor. At about this time he and Wellesz became closer again, partly because of Wellesz's monograph but also because the two men shared this monarchist nostalgia.

Webern, who came from the land-owning class in Carinthia, seems to have voiced some anti-Semitic sentiments – although he had supported his teacher at the time of the Mattsee incident. Schoenberg was aware of this, since in May 1923 he jotted a note to himself referring to Webern's anti-Semitic 'Seipel-phase', a reference to Ignaz Seipel, the xenophobic Christian Socialist Chancellor of Austria through much of the 1920s.

Schoenberg's pre-war friendship with Kandinsky was likewise put to the test by the rumour that Kandinsky had made anti-Semitic remarks.

The war had parted the two – Kandinsky had returned to Russia
at the outbreak of war and remained there during the early post-
revolutionary years. When contact between the two men was
resumed in 1922, Kandinsky was teaching at the Bauhaus in Weimar
and tried to persuade Schoenberg to join the school as Director of
Music. Correctly or not, Alma Mahler (who between 1915 and 1920
was married to Walter Gropius, founder of the Bauhaus) reported to
Schoenberg that there was strong anti-Jewish feeling in the Bauhaus.
When Schoenberg questioned Kandinsky about this, the artist de-
fended himself somewhat clumsily, provoking a long and thoughtful
response from Schoenberg on 4 May 1923. Schoenberg's letter is a
significant document which, not unlike Jakob Wassermann's autobiographical *Mein Weg als Deutscher und Jude* ('My Way as a German
and a Jew'), published a year earlier, identifies the danger of falling,
albeit unwittingly, for anti-Semitic modes of thought:

> *Because I have not yet said that for instance when I walk along the
> street and each person looks at me to see whether I'm a Jew or a Christian,
> I can't very well tell each of them that I'm the one that Kandinsky and
> some others make an exception of, although of course that man Hitler is
> not of their opinion. And then even this benevolent view of me wouldn't
> be much use to me, even if I were, like blind beggars, to write it on a
> piece of cardboard and hang it round my neck for everyone to read. Must
> not a Kandinsky bear that in mind? Must not a Kandinsky have an
> inkling of what really happened when I had to break off my first working
> summer for 5 years, leave the place I had sought out for peace to work in,
> and afterwards couldn't regain the peace of mind to work at all. Because
> the Germans will not put up with Jews! Is it possible for a Kandinsky to
> be of more or less one mind with others instead of with me?*

The words are prophetic, and Schoenberg understood the danger
of Hitler – who was still some ten years away from seizing power –
almost before anyone else in his vicinity. It is possible that the reference to Hitler related to Schoenberg's conversations with Karl Kraus,
for Kraus would publish his first criticism of Mussolini and Hitler
in the following issue of *Die Fackel*, in June 1923.

The social and political climate of post-war Austria and Germany
raised again the old question of identity, although it had clearly not

been absent from Schoenberg's mind during the preceding years. He pointed out to Kandinsky that a belief in a higher being had provided him with solace during the war and this can be linked to the theological subtext of the *Jakobsleiter*. Theosophy and a vision of Swedenborgian heaven are important in the *Jakobsleiter*, although they did not lead Schoenberg towards a state of serene peace: tension and an unresolved inner crisis remain the text's most potent aspects. Back in 1915 Schoenberg had told Zemlinsky that he intended to compose a new symphony that would differ from his recent 'impressionistic' works. He had tried to persuade Richard Dehmel to write a literary programme for such a symphony, but as this came to nothing, Schoenberg undertook to provide the philosophical and literary framework himself and it was this that eventually became the text for the *Jakobsleiter*. After the war the Expressionist writer Franz Werfel, who was living with Alma Mahler and later became her third husband, remarked on reading the *Jakobsleiter* that he understood Schoenberg's inner conflict better, for this was the work of 'the Jew who suffers from himself'. Schoenberg would have disagreed, possibly rightly, but Werfel, a Jew himself, had identified Schoenberg's need to believe and his struggle to give his religious belief adequate expression through his music.

The only new works by Schoenberg that Ravel had heard during his visit to Vienna in 1920 were two piano pieces performed by Eduard Steuermann, which, according to Erwin Stein, impressed the French visitor. Writing to Schoenberg in Zandvoort, Stein regretted that they had not had any new and larger work to show Ravel. Stein, however, was not fully aware of the historical importance of the compositions that Ravel did hear – two of the pieces (Nos. 1 and 2) that later made up the set of the Five Piano Pieces, Op. 23. Like Schoenberg's earlier piano pieces they were short (the longer one just over thirty bars long, the shorter just over twenty); they were atonal and they bore the characteristic stamp of Schoenberg's earlier piano music: carefully planned contrapuntal lines within rhythmically complex, rapidly changing textures. Ravel apparently liked them, said that he understood them, and concluded that no one except Schoenberg could compose like that.

The immediately recognizable traits of Schoenberg's idiom disguised the fact that the process that led to the creation of these piano pieces included a thorough re-examination of his previous approach to composition. Work on the *Jakobsleiter* had made him increasingly aware that the complexity of long, atonal stretches becomes difficult to sustain if one is to persist in presenting moments of pure expression. As had happened before, the working-out of a solution directed Schoenberg towards the piano, since this would force him to employ sparser textures and focus his mind on detail. His earlier essay in this direction had resulted in the Six Little Piano Pieces, Op. 19, which he composed in 1911 within only a few months. The task facing Schoenberg with the new piano pieces required a great deal of analytic and synthetic power, together with a careful structuring of detail. Moreover, the structure of the pieces was no longer to be dictated by pure expression but rather by the need to unite the motivic and harmonic dimensions – so that behind the expressive surface there was logic, accountability and (as he himself said) 'comprehensibility'. Formal patterns, groups of notes interacting with other groups, at times growing, at other times contracting, permeated his new piano textures and – over some three years – led him to what would become known as the twelve-note method. In hearing the two piano pieces Ravel witnessed the beginning of this process without being aware of the real nature of the organization that kept the pieces together. Schoenberg here used sets of notes combined in order to form longer melodic stretches. In the first piece, melodic lines containing as many as twenty-one notes resulted from interlocking three-note motifs, and in the second piece, a series of nine notes became an important structural block. Such compositions, if not yet based on twelve-note rows, could be called 'serial', since they depended on an ordered set (or series) of pitches subjected to permutations similar to those which would become standard in twelve-note compositions.

Since there was a danger that atonal textures would become too chaotic and difficult to control, Schoenberg was drawn to the possibility of using a melodic shape in which each of the twelve notes of the Western chromatic scale (on a keyboard, all white and black keys within an octave) would occur only once until all twelve had been stated. Such a shape, functioning as the basic idea of a composition but avoiding any sense of a prevailing tonal centre, can be subjected to changes and alterations. Thus, a twelve-note melody, or 'row', if played in retrograde (backwards) still results in a closely related pattern, albeit one that appears to the ear as a new melody. Further changes may be obtained by inverting the direction of each of the intervals between the notes of the original pattern (for example, an ascending major third would become a descending one) and then this new shape (inversion) could itself be played in retrograde. In order to derive shorter motifs, the row can also be split into three groups of four notes or four groups of three. More patterns still may be obtained by transposing each of the rows to a different pitch, or by reordering the notes in the original series (for example, by changing the order 1-2-3-4-5-6-7-8-9-10-11-12 into 7-8-9-10-11-12-1-2-3-4-5-6). In the Wind Quintet, Op. 26, written in 1924, the original row contains two almost identical six-note phrases presented a perfect fourth part. Interestingly, once the original row of the quintet is played in its inversion, the three new note groups still retain some of the original individuality since the resulting three four-note motifs contain the groups of notes that had made up the original row but in a changed order (although Schoenberg began using this type of structuring of four-note groups only a few years later):

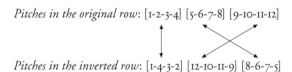

Pitches in the original row: [1-2-3-4] [5-6-7-8] [9-10-11-12]

Pitches in the inverted row: [1-4-3-2] [12-10-11-9] [8-6-7-5]

In other words, shapes derived from the original row are not randomly ordered but represent a varied succession of closely related motifs. Given that instances of inversion as a means of generating new material are often found in the music of Bach, Beethoven and Brahms, it could be said that Schoenberg was only trying to give a rational justification to a long-established detail of the craft of composition.

Compositions built up serially or according to the fully fledged twelve-note principle offered an inner unity, and Schoenberg would later state that the method was there 'for the sake of a more profound logic'. This unity was reminiscent of the idea of a perfect Swedenborgian space in which every detail is related to every other detail and nothing is dissipated. Every musical utterance is forever brought back to itself by the principle of cohesion and conforms to an Idea.

The somewhat pretentious Swedenborgian and theosophical mode of thought was harnessed by Schoenberg to help him produce a work of art that need not be approached from the heights of such philosophical dizziness. Taken on its own terms, the very fabric of this type of composition involved a cross-fertilization between groups of notes, as in the example just quoted from the quintet. In such cases the order even becomes expressible in series of numbers: the traditional Jewish Cabbala (the belief in the power of the abstract numerical principle), which Schoenberg retained even after his conversion to Protestantism, here becomes an aid in shaping the creative inspiration.

At the end of the war Schoenberg became aware that another Viennese composer, Josef Matthias Hauer, had arrived at the idea that music could be organized through permutational patterns of twelve pitches contained within the scale of the Western chromatic octave. The two composers became interested in each other's work and at one point Schoenberg even thought that they might work out some theoretical principles together. However, Hauer was not so intensely compelled by the need to rethink compositional principles and lacked the driving force of Schoenberg's creative imagination, and so they parted. Schoenberg was struck by the importance and the potential of his new organizational method and was torn between the urge to claim the 'discovery' for himself and begin to inform his friends about it, and the desire to keep quiet and work on his new idea undisturbed. Schoenberg recorded that his first communication

Schoenberg tended to be serious in photographs, yet several images from the mid 1920s show him smiling.

Opposite, Schoenberg's
autograph of the Prelude
from his Suite for Piano,
Op. 25. The starting date,
in the upper right-hand
corner, is 24 July 1921,
and the finishing date, at
the bottom, 29 July 1921.

about the new method was to Erwin Stein, while Schoenberg's
student Josef Rufer later claimed that it was to him that Schoenberg
said: 'Today I have succeeded in something by which I have assured
the dominance of German music for the next century.' Although
this claim, as reported by Rufer, was for a long time accepted as fact,
there is something rather too clear-cut about it. The composer's
grandson E. Randol Schoenberg voiced some serious misgivings
about the veracity of the testimony, which Rufer recorded some
thirty-eight years after the event. As Rufer's conversation with
Schoenberg occurred during the tense time after the Mattsee incident,
it is probable that Schoenberg was expressing his anger over his
German identity being challenged at precisely the time that he was
making a significant contribution to German culture. Evidence
to this effect is provided by a letter that Schoenberg wrote to Alma
Mahler in July 1923:

> *I have begun again to work. Something completely new! The German
> Aryans who persecuted me in Mattsee will have this new thing ...
> to thank for the fact that even they will still be respected abroad for
> 100 years, because they belong to the very state that has just secured
> for itself hegemony in the field of music!*

There is a good dose of heavy Schoenbergian irony here as well as
a touch of humour, and if he did say something similar to Rufer,
then it is likely that the irony was lost on him. Interestingly, in
the 1960s, Felix Greissle and Rudolf Kolisch, each remembering
a different occasion, both stated that Schoenberg had made the
'supremacy' claim in their presence.

     It is impossible to establish a clear chronology of Schoenberg's
early serial and fully twelve-note works. Schoenberg himself began
by thinking in terms of several groups of works, but the pieces
that eventually became parts of two different groups, Ops. 23 and 25,
were chronologically intertwined. In any case, several of them, though
brief, took as long as two years to complete. The publication of the
Five Piano Pieces, Op. 23, a six-movement Suite for Piano, Op. 25,
with Baroque dance titles (Prelude, Gavotte, Musette, Intermezzo,
Menuet and Gigue), and the Serenade, Op. 24, for seven instruments
and tenor voice, ended the creative freeze that had been brought

about by the war, by conducting and teaching duties, and by the problems that Schoenberg had had with the *Jakobsleiter*. In 1922 he abandoned the oratorio altogether and, although he toyed in later years with the idea of completing it, it remained unfinished. At this point, after so many years of silence, publishers were eager to get something new from him. In Copenhagen, Wilhelm Hansen became interested in publishing his work and Schoenberg had to placate Emil Hertzka with the promise of two new works as the price for obtaining a partial release from the contract with Universal Edition.

The information about Schoenberg's new works that seeped out would establish his reputation – erroneously – as a dry mathematician who composed according to an abstract rule and was devoid of a 'true' musical imagination. But nothing could be further from the truth. The Five Piano Pieces, Op. 23 contained nuances of expression and textures close to his Expressionist works of around 1911, while the Suite for Piano, Op. 25, by gesturing in the direction of the new neo-classicism, showed that belief in the power of tradition can be expressed through a radically new texture without recourse to the facile pastiche of older styles then becoming popular in Paris. Schoenberg even planted a fleeting, jaunty, Stravinskian phrase in the final movement of the Suite, the Gigue, as if to say: 'Look: I too can be "modern".' The Serenade, Op. 24, despite its novel sound and structure, has a link with *Pierrot lunaire* and displays a parodic, spiky quality – which was Schoenberg's own, highly original version of the sonorities then emerging in the works of some of his younger German contemporaries, such as Paul Hindemith and Kurt Weill, who were influenced by jazz and popular music. These were subtle links with the trends of the time, but Schoenberg's music was also moving towards another radical period – again, new developments beginning as a means of rethinking a previous creative phase.

The extraordinary formal tightness of his serial compositions – their comprehensibility, as Schoenberg called it – was achieved at the price of distancing the new works from the accepted patterns of sound found in most of the music of the preceding decades (apart from a small number of his own earlier works). This was a deliberate withdrawal into the world of uniqueness, as Schoenberg wanted to remove the work   or at least its immediately audible foreground – from its current surroundings and therefore from any grammatical detail that might connect it with a 'content' represented by familiar syntactical references. Schoenberg's withdrawal from a musical idiom that he considered contaminated by the frequent use of predictable melodic or harmonic patterns brought the listeners into a new musical world, as if revealing some long-sought-after truth. Wellesz, writing his book on Schoenberg while these works were in their gestation, was at the time unaware of Schoenberg's first formulation of the twelve-note principle. Nevertheless, he expressed himself as follows: 'For Schönberg has swept away all half-measures and half-truths. He has created a standard which is important for the right appreciation of the general *niveau* of music.' This would provide the basis for the intensely philosophical, critical argument developed by Theodor Adorno, who in the late 1940s proclaimed Schoenberg as the bearer of everything that is progressive in twentieth-century music. However, by attributing historical inevitability to everything Schoenberg did, Adorno unwittingly made the reception of his music more difficult.

The disturbing Mattsee experience of summer 1921 cost the composer several weeks of concentrated work, but he managed to recapture some of the atmosphere of a summer retreat when friends found him a house in Traunkirchen. His return to Vienna in the autumn coincided with several other unsettling events. First, the Society for Private Musical Performances ceased its activities. Then, in October, his mother died in Berlin, where she had been living with her daughter Ottilie and Ottilie's husband Felix Blumauer. On top of this was the usual distraction of teaching. But with 1922 there came encouraging links with the outside world. Milhaud and Poulenc, who had visited Schoenberg in Mödling in January, did so again in August – they were on their way to Salzburg for the founding festival of the International Society for Contemporary Music (ISCM), at which Schoenberg's Second String Quartet was to be performed. Schoenberg was invited to conduct in Copenhagen; in December Furtwängler performed the Five Orchestral Pieces in Leipzig; and in New York Joseph Stransky conducted the first performance of Schoenberg's only finished work of that period, an orchestration of two Bach chorales.

All this improved Schoenberg's finances considerably, despite the staggering post-war inflation. But family life had its ups and downs.

Schoenberg with Francis
Poulenc in Mödling,
August 1922. The
photograph was taken by
Darius Milhaud.

As they had very little income, Trudi and Felix Greissle were still
living with the Schoenbergs, and the shared ménage led to tensions.
After the birth, in March 1923, of a grandson (named Arnold),
Schoenberg lost patience with the young family and insisted that
they leave. This coincided with the disturbing correspondence
with Kandinsky, which had raised the ugly spectre of the Mattsee
experience. The summer holiday at Traunkirchen promised
Schoenberg some much-needed peace and also the opportunity of
talking to Adolf Loos and discussing composition with Webern, Berg
and Rufer. But this was not to be: Mathilde's health had never been
strong and the visitors to Traunkirchen were alarmed to see how weak
she was getting. Her kidneys began to fail, and on 20 September 1923
she had to be moved to a sanatorium in Vienna where she died on
18 October, the Schoenbergs' twenty-second wedding anniversary.

     Whatever memories the Gerstl affair might have left in the marriage,
they were either repressed or genuinely overcome. Significantly, two

years before Mathilde's death Schoenberg had started writing a poem
that he now expanded into a Requiem for his wife – it was never set
to music. In November 1923 he recorded what, to a sceptic, would
have been hallucinations, but what, for him and many of his friends,
were clear signs that Mathilde was speaking to him from the beyond:

> *I was so pleasantly stimulated. Perhaps those from the other side have
> the power to affect our senses and nerves directly just as present bodies do.
> I would say: I had a general feeling as if something were flowing through
> me … Perhaps they have been given the ability to become apparent to us
> while flying by (on some kind of planet). Perhaps it is also merely that
> they think about us?*

Schoenberg was deeply affected by Mathilde's death and lost all
direction. Later he recalled how he took to drink, smoked a lot,
consumed quantities of coffee and took drugs. The Greissles moved
back to be with him and he wrote to Zemlinsky that all the past
tensions between him and the young family had been his fault. In
the same letter he described a quiet family Christmas and a New
Year's Eve that he had spent playing chamber music with friends.
One of these, his former pupil, the violinist Rudolf Kolisch, brought
his young sister Gertrud to the party. Perhaps Schoenberg in his
letter did not dare to communicate his feelings for Gertrud to the
man who was Mathilde's brother, or perhaps there was nothing to
communicate to Zemlinsky at that stage, but in the early months
of 1924 he and Gertrud were often seen together and he had begun
spending days in Vienna without returning home to Mödling.

His presence in Vienna was in fact dictated by the demanding
rehearsals of *Pierrot lunaire* in preparation for an Italian tour that
took him and the ensemble to seven Italian cities. This trip – which
had no political implications – was the sole instance of Schoenberg
being tolerated by a right-wing dictatorship. Mussolini had come to
power the year before, and in the flush of nationalist euphoria the
composers Alfredo Casella and Gian Francesco Malipiero, encouraged
by the flamboyant poet and dramatist Gabriele d'Annunzio, formed
a society for the promotion of new music (Corporazione delle Nuove
Musiche). Unlike the Nazis later, the Italian Fascists were not opposed
to avant-garde art: indeed, some of the pre-war Futurists, glorifying

Schoenberg (right) and
the Greissles: Felix, Trudi
and 'Bubi' Arnold, the
dedicatee of Schoenberg's
Wind Quintet, Op. 26, in
Traunkirchen, 14 September
1923. The photograph was
taken just before Mathilde's
fatal illness.

violence as they did, supported the Fascists. All this was probably
quite outside the concerns of the Austrian visitors, who rejoiced in
the reception they encountered. Having missed earlier performances
of *Pierrot lunaire*, Giacomo Puccini travelled to Florence to hear it
and to meet Schoenberg, for whom he had a very high regard. A few
years earlier he had been disappointed upon hearing the *Gurrelieder*,
and explained to Alma Mahler that he wished to experience
Schoenberg the radical, not Schoenberg the Wagnerian. Their
meeting in Florence was extraordinarily cordial and the composer
Luigi Dallapiccola, who was present, reported that they all noticed
Puccini's pleasure at something Schoenberg said to him. This may
well have been Schoenberg's recalling of the deep impact made on
him twenty years earlier by the orchestration of *La Bohème*.

Schoenberg's second wife, Gertrud Kolisch, in riding gear, 1925. Schoenberg met Gertrud at Christmas in 1923, soon after Mathilde's death, and they were married on 28 August 1924.

The early summer of 1924 continued in an atmosphere of invigorating optimism. *Erwartung*, by now some twelve years in the waiting, was finally performed on 4 June 1924; this was not in Vienna but in Prague, at the closing concert of the second festival of the ISCM. It was conducted by Zemlinsky and sung by Marie Gutheil-Schoder, for whom the part had been written. The composer was warmly greeted by the audience and reports in the German press were appreciative. On 20 July 1924 Schoenberg conducted the first public performance of the Serenade, Op. 24 at the Donaueschingen Festival, which was fast becoming recognized as the central showcase for the presentation of new music. This south German festival had been founded in 1921 with the financial support of Count Max Egon von Fürstenberg, and when Schoenberg thanked the Count for his invitation to the Festival

Schoenberg with Erika
Wagner, the members
of the *Pierrot lunaire*
ensemble and several Italian
friends in front of San Marco
in Venice, April 1924.

he did so in the most deferential terms. Indeed, his belief that the
'old order', upheld by the aristocracy, was preferable to the tensions
of the post-war years was poignantly expressed in a letter to Loos:

> *I had actually hoped to see you in Donaueschingen. It was very nice
> there and would certainly have interested you very much. A festival
> like that, under the aegis of a man who is not doing it as a means of
> becoming anything, but who, because he has always been something
> in himself, is capable of really bestowing honours, further reinforces
> my distaste for democracy and that sort of thing.*

Although the 'almost-monarchist', as Berg had described him, speaks
here with conviction, it would be wrong to assume that he was succumbing to the lure of strong-arm dictatorial politics, the trap that
attracted so many during the 1920s and 1930s. Schoenberg's nostalgia
continued to be touchingly naive, of the kind that was widespread
in Austria and expressed in the often-heard phrase 'our good old
monarchy'. (This is not far from the conversion experienced by the
novelist Joseph Roth who, after his first trip to the Soviet Union,
said that he had gone there a socialist and returned a monarchist.)
    Schoenberg returned to Mödling in August 1924 after a short
break in the Salzkammergut where he stayed with Mitzi Seligmann,
the sister of Gertrud and Rudolf Kolisch. A few days later he informed Zemlinsky and Alma Mahler that he was going to marry
Gertrud. Zemlinsky was hurt, believing that the memory of his
late sister was insulted, and this caused a temporary estrangement
(ironically, only a few years later Zemlinsky too would remarry soon
after his wife's death). Schoenberg's daughter Nuria Nono reports
hearing from her mother that the wedding ceremony in Mödling
was a subdued affair and that the officiating priest pointedly said:
'I haven't yet expressed my condolences at the death of your wife.'
    While Schoenberg's deep affection for Mathilde is beyond doubt,
in public he had been a lonely man, with Mathilde remaining very
much in the background. Now he and Gertrud appeared to relish
their social life and were frequently seen in Vienna's fashionable cafés.
Gertud was lively, witty and communicative, and photographs of
the time often show a smile on Schoenberg's otherwise dark and
stern countenance. Their wedding took place two weeks before the

Otto Klemperer,
Schoenberg, Webern and
Hermann Scherchen at the
Donaueschingen Festival,
July 1924.

composer's fiftieth birthday, for which celebrations were organized
not just by his pupils but also by the city of Vienna, which honoured
him with a reception in the City Hall and a speech by the Social
Democratic Lord Mayor Karl Seitz. This occasion also saw the
performance of the Wind Quintet, Op. 26, which employed the new
twelve-note method even more ambitiously than did Schoenberg's
previous compositions for the piano. Indeed, Op. 26 ushers in a
new compositional phase in which Schoenberg was guided by the
'new formal principles', as Erwin Stein called them in an important essay published in the *Festschrift* for Schoenberg's birthday.

Despite its broader significance, the quintet contains a deeply felt
personal statement – it is, in fact, a work that celebrates those around
him. The score is dedicated to 'little Arnold', his sixteen-month-old
grandson, while on the copy that he presented to Gertrud, he wrote
that although he was thinking of his grandson when he started the
work, he was thinking of her when he was finishing it. Indeed, the

Lilly Steiner's etching intended for the cover of the score of *Erwartung*, made in Prague after the work's first performance and presented by her to Schoenberg for his fiftieth birthday, in 1924. (It was for Hugo and Lilly Steiner that Adolf Loos designed a strikingly modern house in 1910 – see photograph on p. 51.)

closing rondo, though not in any sense descriptive, communicates a sense of joy and lightness that is seldom encountered in Schoenberg's works. At the very end of the rondo a reminiscence of the opening motif of his First Chamber Symphony reinforces the personal feel of the quintet.

The other long-awaited first performance, a staging of the Expressionist *Die glückliche Hand*, took place in Vienna's Volksoper in October 1924 as part of an ambitiously planned, month-long festival to celebrate the city's music and theatre. Finally it looked as though the tide was turning and Schoenberg was beginning to achieve public recognition as the central figure of Vienna's contemporary music scene, an accolade that his admirers considered long overdue. But Viennese intrigue and the bourgeois fear of the new were also alive and well, and the rivalry between the Staatsoper and the Volksoper quickly cut short the run of *Die glückliche Hand*. Moreover, in November 1924 the *Musikpädagogische Zeitschrift*, the organ of the Austrian Federation of Music Teachers, published a very negative review of the work; this precipitated Schoenberg's resignation from the Federation and reinforced his feeling that he was not welcome in Vienna. Schoenberg and Gertrud's honeymoon in Italy in January 1925, evoking the happy memories of the *Pierrot lunaire* tour, brought renewed contacts with Alfredo Casella and Gian Francesco Malipiero and a much-needed change of air from the poisoned atmosphere of Vienna. It is therefore not surprising that Schoenberg again felt the need to move away from the city. In May 1925 an approach came from Alexander Veprik, then at the Moscow Conservatoire, and Schoenberg initially showed some interest. This went no further, but had it done so Schoenberg would probably have suffered a personal tragedy: Veprik himself was lucky to survive years of imprisonment in the Gulags.

Back in 1912 Ferruccio Busoni had toyed with the idea of finding Schoenberg a teaching post at a German institution. With Busoni's death in July 1924, the chair of advanced composition at the Prussian Academy of Arts in Berlin had become vacant, and Schoenberg was approached a year later. Although the idea came from Franz Schreker, the negotiations surrounding the appointment were in the hands of Leo Kestenberg, Busoni's one-time piano pupil and a friend of Scherchen's (Kestenberg was by then an influential music adviser in the Social Democrat-controlled Prussian Ministry of Education). The appointment was prestigious, offering Schoenberg the freedom to shape his own course and select his students from among the most talented. He would be required to teach only six months of the year and yet be guaranteed a comfortable annual salary which would free him from financial constraints for the first time in his life. The preparations proceeded encouragingly smoothly: at the end of August 1925 Kestenberg travelled to Vienna for the signing of the contract and in the middle of September, Schoenberg received a letter from the

Prussian Minister of Sciences, Art and Public Education confirming
his appointment to the professorship with effect from 1 October,
together with his membership of the Senate of the Prussian
Academy of Arts.

'I have been told you wished to publish an interview with me.
I must ask you, however, to abandon this proposal. For it is my most
intense desire to depart from Vienna as unnoticed as I have always
been while I was here. I desire no accusations, no attacks, no defence,
no publicity, no triumph! only p e a c e!' wrote Schoenberg to the
editor of the *Neues Wiener Journal*, who, unsurprisingly, had sought
his reaction to the Berlin appointment. There was a small dose of
irony here, for even if Schoenberg had not been widely known in
Vienna in the early years of the century, this was hardly true by
the mid 1920s. Nevertheless, his desire for peace was genuine, and
reflected his wish to have the space and freedom in which to compose and develop the theoretical aspects of twelve-note composition.
Berlin had already provided him with two beneficial changes of
environment, and this time the prospect of financial security must
have made the German capital seem even more attractive. Although
Schoenberg must have been aware that Germany was beset by
political problems, the country could offer him a broader stage, one
on which he could more easily avoid the harassment and pressures
prevalent in a diminished Austria.

7

A portrait of Schoenberg by
Man Ray, 1927.

*Schoenberg exudes something inexorable and
severe. His irony is harsh, at times even angry.
One doesn't see his small figure, one sees only the
eyes and the mouth – and above them the extremely wide forehead in an enormous baldness,
as if the brow had not had enough space …
The eyes are the strangest thing about him.
They continuously change their disposition.*

Arno Huth,
'Arnold Schoenberg Speaks
– Lecture at the Academy of
Fine Arts in Berlin',
Allgemeine Zeitung (Chemnitz),
5 February 1927

An Uneasy Calm before the Storm
1925-32

There are two opposing views of Weimar Germany, both to a large
extent true. One implies that the first German experiment in parliamentary democracy was doomed from the beginning, since there
was too much tension between the forces of the old order – the army,
the aristocracy and the unreformed imperial bureaucracy – and the
new forces of the political Left, itself riven by conflict between the
revolutionaries and the moderate reformists. The other view claims
that there existed in Germany an abundance of creative talent, despite the political tensions and the appalling financial crisis of 1922–4,
and that the heavy subsidies that the government gave to the arts
created an atmosphere of such vibrant innovation that Berlin (and
several other German cities), rather than Paris, became the focus
of cultural life in Europe. Moreover, once the effects of inflation
were curbed, there were encouraging signs in the mid 1920s of a
greater political stability, which offered some hope for non-violent
political reform. The truth was that the arts were politicized, and
that artistic innovations came overwhelmingly from artists on the political Left, who regarded the established giants of modern German
literature – Thomas Mann, Stefan George and Gerhart Hauptmann
– as anachronisms left over from the Wilhelmine period (the three
decades of Kaiser Wilhelm II). Among the composers, the old guard
was dominated by Richard Strauss and Hans Pfitzner, with the latter
remaining an essentially German figure, deprived of the international
success enjoyed by Strauss.

Schoenberg's monarchist nostalgia was not something that the
new German avant garde – people like Bertolt Brecht, Erwin Piscator
or Kurt Weill – would have accepted or even understood, yet he
had nothing in common with the German conservatives either. He
may have wished for peace and creative space, but the divisions of
Weimar Germany meant that he did not remain unaffected and was
soon pulled into the political stream, albeit against his will. The part
that Leo Kestenberg played in his Berlin appointment did not remain

unnoticed in the press. Like Hermann Scherchen, Kestenberg went through a radical phase in the immediate post-war years as a member of the Independent German Socialist Party and as an organizer of its *Proletarische Feierstunden* (Socialist Mass Celebrations). Moving away from the radical Left, he then joined the Social Democratic Party, whose strength in the Prussian parliament ensured him a government position. This resulted in his ambitious plan for the reform of musical education in Prussia, which was to encompass everything from primary education to the organization of the conservatoires. As an administrator Kestenberg had a broad-minded approach, believing, for instance, that it was right to have the conservative Pfitzner teaching at the Hochschule für Musik, possibly as a counterweight to Schoenberg and Schreker at the Academy. Even though Kestenberg was not interested in the political beliefs of the composers he supported, Schoenberg could scarcely escape being perceived as Kestenberg's man by German conservatives and anti-Semites. The proof came soon enough, when Alfred Heuss – editor of the *Zeitschrift für Musik* and soon to emerge as a founder-member of the Nazi-led Kampfbund für deutsche Kultur (Fighting League for German Culture) – described Schoenberg's appointment as a provocation, a trial of strength between 'Germanness' and the 'Jewish spirit in music'. But although the spectre of hatred had already manifested itself, Schoenberg was probably willing to overlook it since, above all, he understood his appointment to be a long-overdue recognition of his stature as a composer and teacher.

Immediately after signing the Berlin contract, Schoenberg and Gertrud went to Venice for the festival of the ISCM, where Schoenberg conducted his Serenade, Op. 24. The festival also marked the beginning of Schoenberg's long dispute with the Society, whose president, the English musicologist Edward J. Dent, offended him by insisting that he should not exceed the allotted rehearsal time. This incident later grew in Schoenberg's mind; in the years that followed he repeatedly demanded an apology from Dent and, at least in private communications, wanted Dent dismissed from the presidency of the Society.

At the ISCM festival Schoenberg heard Stravinsky play his new Piano Sonata. This encounter with Stravinsky's brand of neo-classicism – which was superficially Bach-like, in a tonal idiom and very different from the style of the works prior to *Pulcinella* (1920) –

seems to have seriously perplexed and annoyed Schoenberg. He saw
in Stravinsky's new conservatism a capitulation, a refusal to think the
task of composition through, and a facile appropriation of stylistic
properties of a past age as though from a box of props. Perhaps, deep
inside, he was also aware that Stravinsky's pastiche was accessible and
demanded less concentration and effort from its listeners than did
the complex textures of his own music. He believed that his twelve-
note method had deep historical roots, but that it involved a dialec-
tical engagement with long-established techniques while avoiding
audible references to the past. And yet, because Schoenberg regarded
the past as deeply embedded in his consciousness, the conjunction
of the pitches B flat–A–C–B, spelling BACH in German notation,
appeared as a not-so-hidden topos in the Suite for Piano, Op. 25, and
reappeared two years later in the Variations for Orchestra, Op. 31.

His first reaction to the Bach à la Stravinsky and other streams of
neo-classicism materialized in the shape of the witty, cruel and rather
angry Three Satires, a choral work he began in November 1925 while
suffering from the appendicitis that delayed his departure for Berlin.
Stravinsky was particularly harshly dealt with:

Well, who then is banging over there?
Why, it's little Modernsky!
He's had his hair cut in a bob;
looks very good!
Like real false hair!
Like a wig!
Just (as little Modernsky imagines him) –
just like Papa Bach!

In the note published with the score, Schoenberg avoided naming
Stravinsky and claimed that his satires were directed against those
who sought to return to the past, those who cultivated a folk-inspired
style, and against 'all "-ists", in whom I can only see mannerists'.
Schoenberg brilliantly captured what he saw as the superficiality
of the new cleverness by casting the 'Modernsky' piece as a perpetual
canon that sounds the same even when sung from the score
turned upside down. A *tour de force* of contrapuntal dexterity,
it was intended to demonstrate that it is not the technique itself that

Gertrud and Arnold
Schoenberg in Venice in
1925, where the previous
year Schoenberg had
stood with the performers
of *Pierrot lunaire*.

matters but rather the expressive ideal behind it – and it was this ideal that Schoenberg believed to be lacking in the music that he set out to ridicule.

This was the first eruption of a deep disagreement between Schoenberg, whose Modernism was still essentially governed by an Expressionist aesthetic, and the younger generation of composers – Kurt Weill, Ernst Toch, Hanns Eisler – who were developing a new aesthetic of distance and alienation, devoid of emotion. Although Brecht did not invent the term 'alienation-effect' (*Verfremdungseffekt*) until 1936, a change in aesthetic became increasingly evident in the new German theatre of Brecht and Piscator (especially after the first performance of Brecht's *Mann ist Mann* in September 1926) and in the music of Kurt Weill. Among Schoenberg's followers, Eisler was the first to express his dissatisfaction with his teacher's twelve-note method. In Eisler's case the dissatisfaction was influenced by the German Communist Party's doctrine (in force since September 1922) that art must be revolutionary propaganda directed at the masses and not a source of pleasure for a limited number of bourgeois connoisseurs.

Hanns Eisler, Schoenberg's most distinguished student after World War I. He retained his admiration for Schoenberg but as a Communist voiced serious criticism of the 'bourgeois' nature of his teacher's art.

But the new technique of distancing was not confined to Communist sympathizers: it could also be found in works by Stravinsky and Hindemith, and – among those close to Schoenberg – in Berg's treatment of the uncomprehending, machine-like character of Wozzeck, who wakes up only slowly to the cruelties of the surrounding world. Yet Berg achieved an alienation effect in a musical idiom that Schoenberg could and did accept, as witness his message to Berg, once he had seen the opera (he missed the première because of his appendix operation). Writing to Berg in January 1926 he was somewhat guarded, saying that there were 'some things' in the work that he did not find good, though he concluded that the opera was impressive and that he could be proud of such a student.

Once again, conflicting pressures began to have an unsettling effect on Schoenberg. He had moved to Berlin to take up a prestigious appointment, only to be attacked by the conservatives as a dangerous innovator who was going to corrupt the greatness of German music. Conversely, some of the younger German composers, attracted by the vitality of popular music and jazz, and influenced by the social criticism that originated in the style of painting called *Neue Sachlichkeit* ('New Objectivity'), which soon spread to other arts, found Schoenberg's continuing pursuit of complexity and symphonic length anachronistic. He was aware of this dichotomy and, when asked in 1928 by the *Musikblätter des Anbruch* to write a contribution for the issue celebrating Franz Schreker's fiftieth birthday, he wrote, somewhat bitterly: 'Dear friend, we both belong to the good old times when those who were not sympathetic to us made themselves known by calling us "the Neutöner". How are we to find our direction now that they call us "the Romantics"?' Schoenberg's earlier opponents were still there, persisting in their rejection of his music, still insisting that it was dissonant or insufficiently German, while some of the younger German composers were exaggerating the differences between themselves and Schoenberg with a zeal that was characteristic of the intellectual climate of the Weimar period, a time when questions of political or artistic group identity loomed large. Since Schoenberg's twelve-note music retained a recognizably Expressionist tension, now combined with the suggestion of clear phrase-structure, it was deemed too different from the newest trends and therefore not in keeping with the spirit of the time. Yet this critical argument was weakened by its failure to recognize the role of individuality as a driving force, succumbing instead to the Weimar malaise of the need to ideologize. Yet Schoenberg, too, in his own way, carried the avant-garde banner, albeit without an openly professed belief in the social relevance of music.

With hindsight, it is possible to see that the Serenade, Op. 24 and the Suite for Piano, Op. 25 involve nothing that is alien to the aesthetics of the time. The problems of comprehensibility in the Wind Quintet, Op. 26 stem partly from the ambitious length of the composition (it lasts over forty minutes) and partly from the rather narrow range of timbral contrasts. By May 1926, when he completed the Suite, Op. 29 for three clarinets, two violins, viola and piano, Schoenberg's

A unified view of the world: (*left*) Schoenberg's design for a ticket on the integrated system of public transport in Berlin, submitted to the Berlin city transport company in 1927, and (*right*) his device for determining the permutations of the twelve-note series for his Wind Quintet, Op. 26.

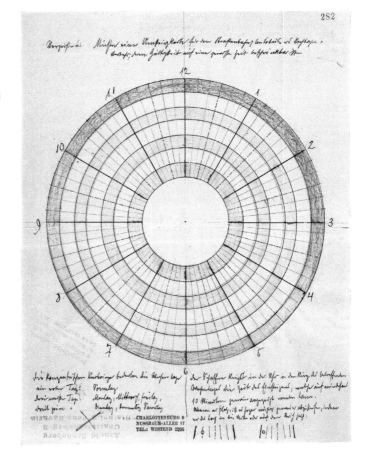

assurance and confidence had grown, resulting in a masterly handling of the twelve-note idiom. Instrumental timbres and textures – which Schoenberg draws from the unusual combination of winds, strings and piano – reveal an aural imagination that would not be surpassed in his subsequent works and distantly presage some sound combinations in Messiaen's, Boulez's and Stockhausen's music of the 1940s and 1950s. Even if the Suite did not intend to offer prescriptive answers to the objections raised by Schoenberg in his Three Satires, the work at least implied them. The sleight-of-hand presence of Friedrich Silcher's folksy melody, *Ännchen von Tharau*, in a sophisticated set of twelve-note variations seems to prove that a popular tune need in no way curb an original imagination or lead to predictable solutions,

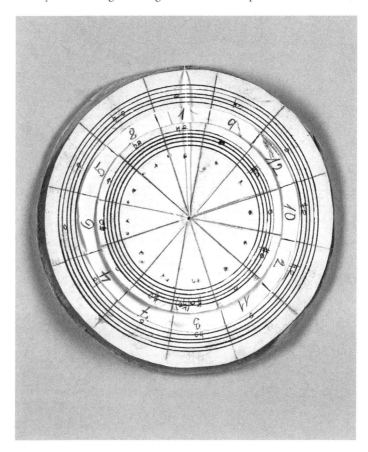

and the Baroque references are sophisticated and veiled, more so than Stravinsky's ready-mades and pastiche. Schoenberg's original idea for the jokey titles of the movements had a Dada flavour – 'Fl. Kschw. Walzer', 'Film Dva', 'Tenn Ski' – and were meant to refer to aspects of Gertrud's character. But in the end he opted for less cryptic titles: 'Ouverture', 'Dance Steps', 'Theme and Variations' and 'Gigue'.

Despite being, arguably, one of the finest examples of both Schoenberg's music and 1920s music in general, the Suite has remained underrated by critics and neglected by performers. Its first performance took place under Schoenberg's direction in Paris – fittingly so, for its spirit brought Schoenberg's idiom closer to the understanding of the Parisian audience than any other of his works except *Pierrot lunaire*. When, after Schoenberg's death, Robert Craft undertook to familiarize Stravinsky with Schoenberg's twelve-note composition, it was significant that he chose this work as his starting point.

Although Schoenberg was familiar with Berlin, the conditions he encountered there in 1926 were very different from those he had known during his previous sojourns. He was now a Prussian state official and therefore much more at the centre of events; the professorship of composition brought with it bureaucratic responsibilities and obliged him to attend the meetings of the Prussian Academy. He was also given Prussian nationality, which terminated the protracted uncertainty over his Austrian citizenship (a problem still unresolved after the break-up of the Dual Monarchy). As always, he took his teaching responsibilities very seriously. Some of his pupils followed him from Vienna, among them Walter Goehr, Walter Gronostay, Roberto Gerhard and Winfried Zillig. In Berlin they were joined by, among others, Josef Zmigrod (who later changed his name to Allan Gray), Nikos Skalkottas and Marc Blitzstein. Josef Rufer became an assistant and gave harmony and counterpoint classes.

Teaching duties once more slowed down Schoenberg's rate of composition, at least initially, and although in March 1926 he complained to Webern that he had not composed much, he completed the Suite, Op. 29 in May and immediately started sketching a twelve-note theme for a set of symphonic variations. His summer break in 1926 was longer than usual: he and Gertrud went first to Dubrovnik in Yugoslavia and then to Pörtschach on the Wörthersee in Austria. He felt he needed a Mediterranean holiday in order to combat his asthma,

which had worsened once again after a cold Berlin winter. This
recurring problem drew him increasingly to the Mediterranean.
The political situation in Germany would soon deteriorate after the
international economic crisis in 1929, with the anti-Semitic Right
and the Nazi party gaining in influence. Schoenberg's frequent
asthma attacks may therefore have been caused by prolonged tension:
certainly they were more than a convenient excuse. So what had
appeared to be an elevation to a prestigious post soon became
a source of apprehension.

Although still nominally a Protestant, Schoenberg was increasingly preoccupied with not just his own Jewish identity but also the
survival and safety of the entire Jewish nation. When, in the early
part of the century, Zionism had emerged in Vienna as a response
to the anti-Jewish sentiments of the Austrian Christian Socialists,
Schoenberg had taken little interest in it, adhering to his belief that
an artist's primary commitment was to his creative work. Although
this belief had been the basis of his objection to Eisler's involvement
with Communism, it did not prevent Schoenberg from moving
towards an engagement with Zionism in the 1920s. His idea of
composing a cantata entitled *Moses and the Burning Bush* was, in a
way, the logical development of his wish to treat the subject of an
individual's quest for self-knowledge – something he had already
tried to do in the *Jakobsleiter* and in the Four Pieces for mixed
choir, Op. 27. His own texts for two of the pieces from Op. 27 were
strongly marked by a Jewish distrust of images, and the opening of
the second poem is particularly telling in this respect:

Thou shalt make unto thyself no image!
For an image restricts,
limits, grasps
that which should remain unlimited and unimaginable.

Drawn now to the biblical episode in which the Ten Command-
ments are handed to Moses, Schoenberg experienced difficulties
similar to those he had encountered with the *Jakobsleiter*. He found
the subject too complex for the limited framework of a cantata, and
expanded the idea into a more elaborate dramatic structure: the
work was now to be an opera, entitled *Moses und Aron*.

Schoenberg with students
in his masterclass in
Berlin (1926/7). Standing
(left to right): Adolph Weiss,
Walter Goehr, Walter
Gronostay, Winfried Zillig,
Max Walter, Josef Rufer
(Schoenberg's assistant);
seated: Schoenberg
and Josef Zmigrod.

Side by side with the grandiose biblical subject for the opera, he devoted himself to writing a literary work which had a decidedly contemporary political theme, the play *Der biblische Weg* ('The Biblical Way'). The story concerns a Jewish idealist called Max Aruns who settles in an area of Africa where a New Palestine has been established (the African location is a clear reference to the idea proposed by the founder of Zionism, Theodor Herzl, that a Jewish state should be established there). Strife and disagreement eventually lead to a rebellion in which Aruns is killed. In his dying moments Aruns admits that his abandonment of the idea and reliance on the secret weapon that he was hoping to develop made him an object of divine retribution. Although the play was not performed in Schoenberg's lifetime, it retains a historical importance as a monument to Schoenberg's particular form of engagement with the Zionist cause – an engagement affirming idealism and warning against the use of force.

The idealist aspirations of both *Moses und Aron* and *Der biblische Weg* contrasted with the prevailing atmosphere in Berlin, where one increasingly lived for the moment. This was evident in the vigorous growth of film, the blurring of boundaries between classical and popular music in the hands of composers such as Hindemith and Weill, and the faith in developing technologies. Schoenberg, it seems, was constantly poised between his own intimate world, craving a withdrawal from modernity, and the need to engage with 'reality'. On an everyday level this was manifest in his participation in the Berlin bar and café culture, which was possibly a direct result of Gertrud's gregariousness.

Following his election to the Prussian Academy, Schoenberg delivered a lecture, in January 1927, which is known under the title of its 1934 English translation – 'Problems of Harmony'. Here, rather than talking about his innovations, Schoenberg addressed the more fundamental issue of the need, as he saw it, for musical structures to keep renewing themselves. Whether wittingly or not, he repeated an argument made in 1854 by the Viennese music critic Eduard Hanslick in his *Vom Musikalisch-Schönen* ('On the Musically Beautiful'). Hanslick was sceptical about the ability of music to transmit narrative content since music, he said, relies solely on its own material:

[t]here is no art which wears out so many forms as quickly as music. Modulations, cadences, intervallic and harmonic progressions all in this manner go stale in fifty, nay, thirty years, so that the gifted composer can no longer make use of them and will be forever making his way to the discovery of new, purely musical directions.

Schoenberg's lecture came remarkably close to this:

An idea in music consists principally in the relation of notes to one another. But every relation that has been used too often, no matter how extensively modified, must finally be regarded as exhausted; it ceases to have power to convey a thought worthy of expression. Therefore every composer is obliged to invent, to invent new things, to present new note relations for discussion and to work out their consequences.

The lecture and the lecturer made a profound impact, and the occasion was reported in the daily press. Schoenberg was not just stating an aesthetic position, he was explaining the very nature of the force that motivates composers 'to invent new things'. Moreover, his listeners were offered an explanation that was valid both for the traditional tonal system and for the twelve-note method.

Schoenberg's own understanding of how to relate various forms of twelve-note sets to one another changed from work to work as he learnt how to shape a composition out of a multitude of derivations from a single twelve-note set. The shaping involved the ability to recognize obvious links (such as the recurrence of identical pitches and intervals) between some forms of series, and to disregard those forms between which links were weaker. He was not interested in mechanical manipulations of the series: rather, his method resembled Beethoven's way of adjusting small details of motivic substance in order to increase their logical coherence. Schoenberg worked his twelve-note series in such a way that, through sensitive handling, they became sources of melodic material and the harmonic web within which they were to be experienced, but without slavish adherence to the repetition of the notes in the series.

Only a few days after his Academy lecture he started working on his Third String Quartet, commissioned by the American patron of new music, Elizabeth Sprague Coolidge. Nearly twenty years had elapsed since Schoenberg's Second String Quartet, and his return to the form in 1927 coincided with a surge of renewed interest in the quartet as a medium for trying out new compositional principles. Berg's *Lyric Suite* had been completed in the previous year; in 1927 Bartók wrote his third quartet after a gap of some ten years; Janáček's remarkable second quartet, *Intimate Letters*, came in 1928. If anything, Schoenberg was less experimental than Berg or Bartók as far as the outward shape of the quartet was concerned. He followed the classical four-movement structure and, especially in the first and last movements, retained phrase-shapes redolent of tonal music, albeit embedded in a sophisticated serial context. He offered the intriguing explanation that the ostinato figure that persists through most of the first movement was suggested to him by an image he had carried in his mind since his childhood. Like most youngsters of his generation, he had been fascinated by Wilhelm Hauff's fantastic stories, particularly the one featuring the captain of an accursed ship whose crew have nailed him through the forehead to the mast. During the day, the crew and the captain appear to be dead, but at night they come to life.

The Kolisch Quartet, champions of Schoenberg's music in the 1920s and 1930s (left to right): Jenö Lehner, Felix Kuhner, Benar Heifetz and the leader, Rudolf Kolisch, Schoenberg's brother-in-law. A childhood injury to his right shoulder forced Kolisch to hold the violin in his right hand and the bow in his left.

It is curious that Schoenberg chose to resurrect this image only now, since it would have fitted in both with the restless nocturnal chase of Waldemar's men in the *Gurrelieder* and the gruesome cruelty depicted in *Pierrot lunaire*.

Writing to Alban Berg in September 1927, Theodor Wiesengrund Adorno, then an ambitious critic as well as Berg's promising student of composition, described Schoenberg's treatment of the serial principle in the quartet as mechanical, and with a rather transparent sycophancy praised Berg's superior craft. Here, Adorno was simply wide of the mark, having mistaken regularity of rhythmic structure for application of the series. This was an early manifestation of the distrust between the composer and the critic that would assume much larger proportions in the 1940s. Adorno and Schoenberg never hit it off from the first, and as early as 1925 Adorno complained that during their first meeting Schoenberg talked to him 'as Napoleon might have talked to a young adjutant'. Adorno remained fascinated, even obsessed, with Schoenberg's music but found the man difficult; Schoenberg found Adorno's prose impenetrable and was far less enthusiastic about his compositions than was his teacher Berg. When, in 1933, Adorno approached Schoenberg for a reference in the hope of obtaining a teaching position in Prussia, he duly obliged, but was lukewarm: 'I do not consider W[iesengrund] to be a composer, but it is indisputable that he has what it takes to be a teacher, and there can be no doubt about the level of his ability.'

Another important contemporary with whom Schoenberg had difficulty in establishing a good relationship was Otto Klemperer. It may be that Klemperer bore Schoenberg a long-standing grudge, for Schoenberg had been somewhat reserved about Klemperer's incidental music for Max Reinhardt's production of *Oresteia* that he had shown him when they first met in 1911. Now Klemperer was a force to be reckoned with as a champion of new music, and, as the Director of the Kroll Opera, he was in a position to bring Schoenberg's works to the stage. However, the music of the Viennese avant garde did not appeal to him and he felt instinctively closer to Stravinsky, Hindemith and Krenek: he approved of the *Neue Sachlichkeit* style while Schoenberg distrusted it. It was the otherwise conservative Wilhelm Furtwängler who first showed an interest in Schoenberg's latest composition, the Variations for Orchestra, Op. 31. Having heard about the work from

Erwin Stein before it had been completed, Furtwängler asked
Schoenberg to let him conduct the first performance. Schoenberg
wrote to Furtwängler, in September 1928, from Roquebrune-Cap-
Martin, one of his favourite Mediterranean resorts, to tell him that
the score was finished. The work was rehearsed in November, and
although at first Schoenberg did not particularly like Furtwängler,
he admitted to Webern that he was a 'good man'. The work's first
performance in December 1928 was yet another occasion when
Schoenberg's music was met by an initial lack of comprehension
on the part of the conservative critics and public alike, accustomed
as they were to the standard repertoire of the Berlin Philharmonic.
The Variations was the first twelve-note work to be written for a symphony orchestra, and the novelty of the idiom at first obscured the
fact that it was a wonderfully inventive showpiece for the orchestra,
predating Bartók's now more popular Concerto for Orchestra by
fifteen years. Moreover, one of the Variations is arguably the best
demonic scherzo that Shostakovich never quite managed to write!

Impressed by the Variations for Orchestra, Klemperer began to
show more interest in Schoenberg's music; he is also likely to have
been influenced by the favourable reception of *Die glückliche Hand*
in Germany earlier in the year. When he heard the rumour that
Schoenberg was working on a new opera (soon to materialize as
Von heute auf morgen), he enquired at Universal Edition, but the
publishers had as yet no knowledge of it. Klemperer had already
conducted Hindemith's *Cardillac* and was particularly keen on
Stravinsky bringing *The Soldier's Tale* and the new *Apollo* to Berlin
in autumn 1928. Schoenberg was only too aware that several of his
contemporaries were gaining instant success with the public, and

Schoenberg wrote that
this image from Wilhelm
Hauff's fantastic tale
Gespensterschiff ('A Ship
of Ghosts') was on his mind
when he composed the
opening of the Third String
Quartet (1927). The
illustration reproduced here
comes from an 1878 edition,
which may have been the
one Schoenberg knew in
his childhood.

although he deeply disapproved of neo-classical pastiche and hybrid
works that attempted to blend the classical idiom with jazz (such as
Krenek's *Jonny spielt auf*), he was convinced that, without compro-
mising his standards and beliefs, he, too, could produce his own
version of a *Zeitoper* (opera on a contemporary subject), which would
bring him success and, of course, good royalties. Hiding behind
the pseudonym of Max Blonda, Gertrud wrote a libretto entitled
Von heute auf morgen ('Here Today, Gone Tomorrow'). As the
expectation of substantial royalties made Schoenberg demand
a rather large fee from Hertzka's Universal Edition, Hertzka declined

Wilhelm Furtwängler in the 1920s. Despite his conservative taste, he showed some interest in Schoenberg's music.

to publish the work. Schoenberg then, unwisely, rejected a good offer from the publishers Bote & Bock and decided to have the score printed at his own expense – an excursion into publishing which proved to be a disaster. Neither he nor Gertrud had any experience in such matters and, instead of securing a good income, Schoenberg ended up by having to subsidize the printing. Klemperer, however, liked the libretto and wanted the work for the Kroll Opera, so when

Erich Kleiber and various other conductors asked to perform it, Schoenberg held back, feeling that he was obliged to Klemperer. But Klemperer, who was erratic and tended to violent mood swings and changes of opinion, then declined *Von heute auf morgen*, although he agreed to conduct *Die glückliche Hand* at the Kroll as a part of a double bill with *Erwartung* (conducted by Zemlinsky). Klemperer next became dissatisfied with *Die glückliche Hand*, too, declaring that Schoenberg had no idea of theatre, and the work was dropped.

In the end *Von heute auf morgen* had its première in Frankfurt in February 1930 under Hans Wilhelm Steinberg, and later in the month Schoenberg conducted a radio performance in Berlin. The fact that the protagonists are nameless (Husband, Wife, a Friend, the Singer) betrays a link with pre-war Expressionist theatre, although the set-ting is vaguely contemporary. The similarity of Schoenberg's title with Georg Kaiser's well-known Expressionist play *Von morgens bis mitternachts* ('From Morn to Midnight', 1912) is probably fortuitous. The simple story revolves around some flirtation during a night out that the Wife and Husband have enjoyed with a Singer and Friend respectively. This leads to tension when the couple return home; the Singer and the Friend then turn up, and the Husband and the Wife realize that their visitors crave only the latest fads (those that last only from one day to the next, as the work's title implies) whereas their relationship, based on genuine love, represents an enduring quality. *Von heute auf morgen* was the first twelve-note opera, and the disparity between its light libretto and complex score proved to be too great to ensure its lasting success. Adorno, in contrast to Berg and Klemperer, both of whom liked the libretto, objected to its 'crassly bourgeois and arch-reactionary' subject, while the public, naturally, preferred the more easily accessible music of Krenek and Weill.

Film was an important ingredient of Weimar culture and the Schoenbergs became avid visitors to Berlin cinemas. At around the time when *Von heute auf morgen* was performed, Schoenberg had another work ready, *Begleitungsmusik zu einer Lichtspielszene* ('Accompaniment to a Film Scene'), the storyline of which is only indicated through the titles of the piece's three sections: 'Menacing danger', 'Anguish' and 'Catastrophe'. Several German Dada artists had experimented with the combination of music and abstract film, and in the early 1920s Hans Richter and Walter Ruttmann, among

A scene from the performance of *Die glückliche Hand* in Breslau (now Wrocław), March 1928. The sets were designed by the noted progressive painter Hans Wildermann, whose work featured in the Nazi exhibition of 'degenerate art' in 1937.

others, made some attempts in this direction. Schoenberg's new work coincided with the appearance of the first sound films in the late 1920s, and he even drafted a short manifesto about the role of music in the sound film in which he envisaged the synthesis of the moving image, language and music in the manner of a new *Gesamtkunstwerk*, to use Wagner's term for this concept.

Begleitungsmusik was Schoenberg's first twelve-note work seriously to appeal to Klemperer, who offered to perform it at the Kroll Opera. He suggested to Schoenberg that László Moholy-Nagy should be asked to devise an abstract film to go with it, but Berg thought that Schoenberg should do this himself. As the lighting at the Kroll for the performances of *Die glückliche Hand* and *Erwartung* had not been to his liking, Schoenberg was sceptical about the suggestion and wrote to Klemperer that he did not know Moholy-Nagy. This was surprising given that Moholy-Nagy, after leaving the Bauhaus in 1928, had become one of Berlin's leading progressive artists. Had he produced the proposed film, however, the result would have been a remarkable collaboration between two highly original artistic minds.

Various radio stations in Germany, especially those in Berlin and Frankfurt, were active promoters of music and many composers readily responded to these opportunities. Hindemith, Weill and Schreker had been quick to realize the value of broadcasting, while Schoenberg, not surprisingly, was initially put off by its over-popular nature and poor quality of sound. But in only a couple of years he moved from his critical position of 1928 and became quite enthusiastic about radio's possibilities. He particularly valued the dispassionate nature of a radio broadcast that presented unfamiliar music away from the concert hall where audience hostility might influence a work's reception. Furthermore, the radio created its own culture of rehearsal, fostering an awareness of the need to iron out small deficiencies before a live broadcast. Schoenberg saw a further possibility: the radio could act as a forum where the composer might meet his critics. In April 1930 he suggested a scenario for such a conversation to Hans Flesch, the head of Radio Berlin, in which he specified the length of the contributions and their order of presentation:

The Universum Cinema in Berlin, designed by Erich Mendelsohn, completed in 1928. Now home of the Schaubühne am Lehniner Platz, it was originally a representative cinema for UFA, one of the major film companies of the time. Schoenberg often attended film premières here and wrote his *Begleitungsmusik zu einer Lichtspielszene* ('Accompaniment to a Film Scene') shortly after the cinema's opening.

Wassily and Nina
Kandinsky with Gertrud
and Arnold Schoenberg
in Pörtschach, 1927. This
was their first meeting
after the tension between
Schoenberg and Kandinsky
in 1923.

First, three critics speak for three minutes each, text to be well defined,
written down, about one and a half typewritten pages. After this the
composer: a response. Likewise a written text (the critics' scripts to have
been shown to him previously for scrutiny), about five to six minutes.
Thereafter a free discussion … The whole thing lasts barely half an hour.

At Radio Berlin they were thinking about something similar, and
the first discussion, between Schoenberg and the writers and critics
Heinrich Strobel and Eberhard Preussner, with Flesch chairing the
event, took place on 30 March 1931. By then Schoenberg had some first-
hand experience of radio behind him, not only in Germany but also
in London, where he had conducted *Erwartung* for the BBC in January
1931. Only a few days before the Berlin radio discussion he had given
a lecture on Radio Frankfurt about his Variations for Orchestra and,
judging from Karl Holl's unusually sympathetic review in the
Frankfurter Zeitung, it appeared that Schoenberg's trust in the radio

was justified. The broadcast had offered him a chance to present a personal view of the work illustrated by musical examples and to talk about his music in more general terms. Discussion in a broadcasting studio, involving authors and critics and usually reserved for the late evening hours, soon became a frequently used format. So Schoenberg the forward-thinking composer was also a pioneer of a now widespread form of communication.

At the end of the academic year 1931, the Schoenbergs went for a prolonged stay at Territet-Montreux in Switzerland. It was to be a recuperative holiday, for Gertrud had not been feeling well and Schoenberg's asthma was badly affected by the Berlin climate; he also had a persistent cough which, like the asthma was not helped by his heavy smoking. He joked that he could give up drinking, but that smoking was too much a part of him to be easily abandoned. The summer, however, turned out to be cool and rainy, and there was no improvement in his health. Originally, he had hoped to finish his new opera *Moses und Aron* before going back to Berlin, but he became aware that the task he had set himself was, as ever, very ambitious. Composition proceeded slowly and by August he had completed only the first act and started on the second. A return to Berlin would interrupt all this, so – after consulting his former pupil, the Catalan composer Roberto Gerhard – the Schoenbergs decided to move to Barcelona for a while, informing the Academy in Berlin, that his doctors recommended a longer period in a warm climate. In October they were in a house in Baixada de Briz No. 14 (now Nos. 20–22; an adjacent part of the street has been renamed Carrer d'Arnold Schönberg). From here he wrote to Berg that they had had to equip the household from scratch, but that the low cost of living in Spain made it affordable. He tried to persuade Berg to join them so that they could spend time exchanging ideas, but Berg, constantly beset by family problems, could not tear himself away from Vienna.

Although Spain had long been experiencing a political crisis, the beginning of 1931 brought an increased hope of stability. Catalonia was for the first time granted limited self-government, and in the whole province, particularly Barcelona, a feeling of euphoria prevailed. Schoenberg's temporary residence in the centre of Catalan culture was welcomed not only by Gerhard but also by Schoenberg's old

A 1930s view of the villa at Baixada de Briz 14 (now 20-22), where the Schoenbergs lived during their stay in Barcelona (October 1931-May 1932). The villa is now dwarfed by surrounding tall buildings.

acquaintance, the cellist, Pablo Casals. So even though Barcelona did not have a magic cure for Schoenberg's asthma, the change of scene, as had often happened before, initially brought with it a renewal of creative energy. Schoenberg also enthusiastically took up tennis and Gertrud later recalled that physical exercise tended to improve his asthmatic breathing. In 1929, in Berlin, he had written a new piano piece, Op. 33a, and now in Barcelona he added another one, Op. 33b, which took him only two days to write. Henry Cowell, the American experimental composer who had been at Schoenberg's Berlin seminar, published the score of Op. 33b in his series *New Music Edition* – a timely appearance of a work of Schoenberg's in the United States, as it turned out, although its composer could not have known that the piece would precede his arrival there by less than two years.

In January 1932 Schoenberg complained to Berg about his poor state of health and lack of progress with the opera: 'I seem to be a bit overworked and that makes me very ill-tempered.' There were also 'articles that turned out badly, countless "diary pages"' (theoretical, personal, etc.)'. All this betrays Schoenberg's restlessness in Barcelona, rather than the calm he had hoped for; he was also showing signs of some deep dissatisfaction, although its cause has never been clearly identified. The likely explanation is that news of the growing tension between the political Left and Right in Germany was increasing his sense of foreboding and anxiety. At the same time, Gertrud was around five months pregnant and this raised concern about her ability to travel back to Germany. Added to all this, Josef Rufer alerted him to the Academy's displeasure over his long absence; Schoenberg tried to explain his reasons to Kestenberg, providing medical certificates from doctors in Spain and Switzerland.

In the spring of 1932 Webern came to Barcelona and conducted a performance of the *Begleitungsmusik*. This visit provided a much longed-for substitute for the composers' past meetings in Austrian holiday resorts, a cherished time in which ideas were exchanged and work discussed. Now the past and the present became curiously intertwined. Webern's visit may have brought some encouragement, but only a few days later came the alarming news from Germany that the Nazis had enormously increased their representation in the Prussian parliamentary elections. Nevertheless, the gloom was dispelled by the birth to the Schoenbergs of a daughter, Dorothea Nuria, on 7 May. The second, characteristically Catalan name was given as a reminder of her birthplace.

On 1 June 1932, one month after Nuria's birth and following an absence of almost a year, the Schoenbergs returned to Germany in a very modern way: they flew with Lufthansa from Barcelona to Stuttgart. In Germany there was very little to rejoice about. The economy had been in a state of rapid decline since the collapse of the New York Stock Exchange in 1929, unemployment was high, and in his increasingly menacing speeches Hitler blamed the Jews and the Communists for all of Germany's economic ills. Schoenberg's response to this political climate was reminiscent of his attempt at creating a stable working environment at the time of Austria-Hungary's collapse in 1918. He began to put in order all his literary production to date and informed Berg in September that it amounted to some 1,500 printed pages, excluding the *Harmonielehre*. But it was impossible to hide from the realities of life and in the same letter he told Berg about his 'depression, no doubt related to my life in Berlin,

Roberto Gerhard's mother and wife, Schoenberg, Roberto Gerhard and Gertrud Schoenberg in Barcelona, towards the end of 1931.

which robs me of all pleasure in my work'. Dating also from about this time is a note, with an ending added by Schoenberg a year later, in which he described the anomalous position in which he found himself. Just as Mahler had defined his loneliness in terms of the exclusion he felt on cultural, national and racial levels, so Schoenberg defined his position as that of a man who was nowhere at home: German nationalist musicians saw him as an internationalist, the National Socialists considered him a Cultural Bolshevik, the Communists rejected him as a bourgeois, the anti-Semites saw a Jew in him, yet the composers he considered closest to him were predominantly Aryans.

In Barcelona, Schoenberg had found it increasingly difficult to give adequate musical substance to the complex dramatic and symbolic content that he envisaged for *Moses und Aron*. So despite his earlier intimations that he would finish the opera by the time of his

return to Berlin, only two out of the three acts had been completed
by March 1932, and the third act eluded him for the rest of his life.
When the incomplete opera was first staged in 1957, it became clear
that the two finished acts made perfect sense by themselves. The
opera is an epic work, exploring questions of religious and meta-
physical significance as well as Schoenberg's constant preoccupation
with the relationship between art, expression and language. Moses
and Aaron (Aron in Schoenberg's spelling), despite being at the centre
of the plot, are not the dominant voices: it is the chorus that provides
the focus of the crucial scenes and the orchestra that carries the most
significant aspects of the musical content – the principle of developing
variation here being executed on a gigantic scale.

The only compositional projects that Schoenberg now pursued
had considerable symbolic significance in the context of current
political upheaval. The proximity of Casals in Barcelona had given
Schoenberg the idea of reworking a harpsichord concerto by the
eighteenth-century Austrian composer Georg Matthias Monn into
a cello concerto. A few months later, after Hitler's rise to power, he
began to recompose Handel's Concerto Grosso, Op. 6, No. 7 as a
concerto for string quartet and orchestra. In these two works he
avoided the modernizing pastiche à la Stravinsky, yet they are not
mere transcriptions. The Concerto after Monn has an elaborate and
demanding cello part, while the orchestral accompaniment is more
complex than an eighteenth-century concerto would have required.
Here, as well as in the reworking of Handel's Concerto Grosso,
Schoenberg altered aspects of Handelian style, which the two models
shared. He condensed long portions of repetitive and sequential
passages that, in his teaching, he often singled out as the weaknesses
of Handelian style. He considered the unvaried repetition as detri-
mental to the process of developing variation, the technique that he so
valued in Beethoven's and Brahms's music. He now seemed to wish
to hold on to German music of the past, defying the political forces
that were conspiring to rob him of that past.

German democracy was in its last, desperate phase; the parliamentary system failed to protect civil liberties, and on 20 July 1932,
five weeks after the Schoenbergs returned to Berlin, the Chancellor,
Franz von Papen, ill-advisedly dismissed the legal Prussian
Social Democratic government. The Nazi party and Nazi-inspired

organizations were encouraged by this and began to organize themselves in the hope of taking over government. Meanwhile, the Left continued to be weakened by the traditional animosity between the reformist Social Democrats and the revolutionary Communists. The solution to the situation, which the conservative élites thought would lead to some stability, was to invite Hitler to form the next government. In 1923 Schoenberg had raised the worrying question of what would happen if Hitler ever came to power; together with millions of Germans, he was now about to get his answer.

8

Schoenberg with his dog
outside his new home in
Brentwood, California.

*America may well consider herself fortunate
to have so distinguished a composer and
teacher choose this country for his home …
Furthermore, it will once more prove to
Germany our intense disapproval of its
tyranny and bigotry. Germany's loss will
be this country's great musical gain.*

George Gershwin,
quoted in *The New York Times*,
26 September 1933

Into Exile 1933–44

During the weeks following the Nazi takeover on 30 January 1933, Schoenberg's public appearances were those of a lecturer, first on 12 February on Radio Frankfurt and then three days later in Vienna, where he repeated a lecture previously delivered in Prague in 1930. The Frankfurt lecture, a brilliant reassessment of Brahms, was later to become widely known under its English title 'Brahms the Progressive'. The second, known as 'New Music, Outmoded Music, Style and Idea', dealt with issues that were fundamental to Schoenberg's aesthetics and understanding of music history. Both would exert their influence upon generations of composers and critics. This, as it turned out, was Schoenberg's last visit to Vienna and the last time that he saw Berg.

Meanwhile, the atmosphere in Berlin was changing rapidly. Only a week into the new regime, Paul Graener, a colleague of Schoenberg's at the Academy, attended a concert at which he protested against the playing of a string quartet by the Jew Maximilian Jarczyk. Graener would soon be appointed vice-president of Goebbels's Reichsmusikkammer (State Chamber of Music). However, on this occasion the members of the Senate of the Prussian Academy were still able to express their indignation at their colleague's action. But this was to be the old Academy's last gasp, for the leadership had passed from Max Liebermann, a Jew, now undesirable, to the conservative composer Max von Schillings. The Reichstag fire of 27 February 1933, blamed by the Nazis on their opponents and used as a pretext for witch-hunting, had only just occurred when Schillings declared that the Jewish influence in the Academy must be brought to an end – and this was before the introduction of the Enabling Act that provided the legal basis for dismantling the old order. Schoenberg attended the meeting at which Schillings spoke, but did not stay until the end. Only days before the Reichstag fire he had written to Pablo Casals about his Cello Concerto after Monn and the letter in no way suggested that it might have been written in a tense situation.

And even after Schillings's announcement, Gertrud wrote optimistically to her sister, describing everyday family life and their plans for the summer.

Many Germans still thought that the Nazis were simply overreacting and that the storm would blow over; others were feeling their way more carefully. In March 1933 Furtwängler had protested in the *Vossische Zeitung* against the removal of Jewish artists, but Berg came out of a lecture given by the conductor in Vienna on 17 May with the sense that Furtwängler had sounded like a Nazi. A couple of days earlier Hindemith (who would later hedge his bets over whether to stay in Germany) suggested to Berg, when they met at Wellesz's house in Vienna, that he should move to Berlin and teach at the Hochschule. Berg found this suggestion preposterous given his artistic reputation and Social Democratic sympathies, but Hindemith seemingly remained unaware of the absurdity of the idea. The Schoenbergs had been contemplating their next move and were finally persuaded of the need to go when, in March, Rudolf Kolisch telegraphed them from Florence suggesting a 'change of air'. On 17 May, the very day of Furtwängler's lecture, the Schoenbergs went to Paris with two small suitcases – Schoenberg had used the pretext of seeing to some publishing business in Paris to ask the Academy for leave of absence. This was granted in a politely official letter, with a sinister final sentence:

Honoured Colleague!

The Minister for Science, Art and Education has empowered me by virtue of the decree U I No. 51950, of 17 May 1933, to grant you leave of absence, with immediate effect, from your position as the Director of a Master School in Musical Composition. The Minister has reserved the right to make further dispositions.

Yours respectfully, Max von Schillings

By September 1933, the family had transferred from Paris to Arcachon, and this leave of absence had become a full dismissal. But in the meantime Schoenberg had taken an important public step, confirming his earlier private sentiments: on 24 July in Paris he was formally

Schoenberg, Nuria and
Gertrud. This photograph
appeared in the *Los Angeles
Times* of 13 December
1934, reporting on the
arrival of the Schoenberg
family in California.

readmitted to the Jewish faith which he had left in 1899. This was
a defiant return to a religious and cultural community that he had
never left emotionally. At about this time he changed the spelling
of his surname from Schönberg to Schoenberg and abandoned the
traditional longhand German style, known as the *Sütterlinschrift*,
in favour of the Roman hand. The local anti-Semitism he had
encountered many years before at Mattsee still loomed large in
Schoenberg's consciousness, enabling him to comprehend the full
seriousness of the danger facing European Jewry. Feeling that the
circumstances now required political action, he seriously considered abandoning music to devote himself to founding a United
Jewish Party and securing a national homeland for the Jews. He
approached several distinguished figures in the Jewish diaspora
but was disappointed by the lack of urgency with which his ideas
were met. Significantly, he did not neglect composition, but could
not think of continuing with *Moses und Aron* while he was in
France during the summer; reworking Handel's Concerto Grosso
proved to be a more manageable task.

On 17 September 1933 *The New York Times* announced that
Schoenberg was coming to teach at the Malkin Conservatoire
in Boston. He had considered that a move to the United States
would be prudent, his first idea being that he might find a rich
patron. But Joseph Malkin's plan was to bring him over as a
teacher, and in the American press there was the expectation that
young American composers would flock to study with him.
George Gershwin even undertook to raise a scholarship fund for
Schoenberg's future students. The Schoenbergs left France on
25 October on the liner *Île de France* and arrived in New York six
days later. Fifteen years after the demise of the Austro-Hungarian
Monarchy the absurdities of the old bureaucratic Kakania still
pursued them. Having been stripped of his German citizenship
following his dismissal from the Berlin post, Schoenberg had to cling
to the fact that his father, Samuel Schönberg, had been domiciled
in the once Hungarian Pozsony. As Pozsony was now Bratislava,
in Czechoslovakia, the Czechoslovak Embassy in Paris issued him
with a passport that enabled him to enter the United States as
a Czechoslovak citizen. This he remained until his naturalization
as a US citizen in 1941.

Several concerts and receptions were organized in Schoenberg's honour, but the New York climate worsened his asthma to such an extent that – a mere ten days after his arrival – he had to cancel a reception at Harvard. Health became a major issue, and as he had to teach in both Boston and New York City, the commuting drained his energy so seriously that more engagements had to be cancelled later in November and December. Moreover, the students who enrolled at the Malkin Conservatoire turned out to be unpromising. The Conservatoire was a new venture, and in order to attract students Malkin relied on the reputation of Schoenberg and several other teachers whom he engaged. However, for gifted students the attraction of such long-established institutions as the Juilliard School or the Ivy League universities was stronger. Schoenberg, unable to continue his composition seminars at the level he had established in Berlin, had, instead, to follow a less demanding programme, based on the one he had devised for the Schwarzwald School in 1918. The poor response may also have been due to the fact that modernity in music in America tended to be synonymous with Paris and Nadia Boulanger. Furthermore, the basis for an understanding of the cultural and emotional components of early twentieth-century German Modernism was absent. It is true that on the East Coast Schoenberg's chamber music was known before his arrival, but the circle exposed to it turned out to have been too small. Given all of this, and bearing in mind his own musical idiom, Gershwin's public support for Schoenberg is all the more remarkable.

The engagement at the Malkin Conservatoire came to an end in May 1934, and in the summer a welcome escape from the humidity of New York became possible when Schoenberg was offered a period of residence in the artistic colony at Chautauqua in New York State. This was a true summer retreat, since he was not obliged to teach. At Chautauqua he came into contact with Ernest Hutcheson and Alfred Stoessel, who were teaching at the Juilliard School, and in a letter to Rudolf Kolisch, Schoenberg expressed the hope that a post for him might be found there for the next academic year. But the salary offered proved to be inadequate, and for the same reason he had to decline a post at a conservatoire in Chicago, where, additionally, the climate would have been no better than in New York. American universities were only just recovering after the general

financial collapse of 1929, and the efforts made on Schoenberg's behalf
by Carl Engel (who was the president of Schirmer, music publishers in
New York) to arrange a profitable lecture tour led nowhere.

Schoenberg put a brave face on this unpromising situation,
especially in his letters to relatives and friends in Austria. He wrote
to Kolisch from Chautauqua: 'For all that, we aren't at all worried.
Sooner or later there will be a publisher for the concertos, which are
bound to be a great success.' The concertos he had in mind were, of
course, the Cello Concerto after Monn and the Concerto for String
Quartet and Orchestra after Handel, but besides the transcriptions
he could also have been referring to a piano concerto for which he
made some sketches in 1933 and the Violin Concerto on which he was
working in earnest at the time. Otherwise, a glance at the chronological list of his works reveals a slowing-down during his last period
in Germany, even before exile caused a much more profound dis-
ruption. Schoenberg's determination to keep on composing showed
itself not so much in finished major works, but in a great number
of fragments and, harking back to the learned tradition of the
Renaissance and Baroque, to ingenious canons based on contrapuntal and notational subtleties which he composed as occasional
pieces and greetings to friends.

Although not conceived at the same time, the two finished major
works of his early American period, the Violin Concerto, Op. 36,
and the Fourth String Quartet, were interleaved chronologically.
The Violin Concerto occupied him between September 1934 and
September 1936, while he completed the quartet in a relatively short
period – three months in the spring and summer of 1936. A spectral
presence of tonal allusions is common to both works and these radiate
through a melodic and harmonic foreground that is dominated by
the twelve-note procedure. The first movement of the concerto has
recognizable traits of the tonic-dominant polarity that is required of
a tonally based sonata structure, yet here they are reduced to a delicate
hint so as not to make the texture hybrid or retrospective. This was
Schoenberg's first essay in original concerto writing, and it involved
the same determination to divest the music of everything that is
merely repetitive and reducible to a pattern. Virtuoso concertos of
the nineteenth and early twentieth centuries contained predictable
idiomatic figurations and scale and arpeggio passages that were on the

whole unrelated to the thematic substance of the work; Schoenberg on
the other hand set out to free the texture of his Violin Concerto from
any such material by concentrating on the substantive and the thematic.

The work had to wait some four years to be heard for the first time,
by which time Berg's Violin Concerto, completed in 1935, had
become better known. The two concertos, both first performed by
the American violinist Louis Krasner, are masterpieces of the
twentieth-century repertoire. Although, on first hearing, Schoenberg's
concerto may seem to lack some of Berg's lyricism, the writing for
solo violin is superior to Berg's in its use of the instrument's sonorities
and in the structuring of the dialogue between soloist and orchestra.
At the first performance of Schoenberg's concerto, in Philadelphia
in December 1940, Krasner and the conductor Leopold Stokowski had
to endure protests reminiscent of those in Vienna some thirty years
earlier. The American public, accustomed to the mainstream classical
and Romantic repertoire, was not yet ready for Schoenberg's music,
and the dismissive phrases of reviewers who wrote for a general
readership had the flavour of the old Viennese invectives: *Time*
magazine, for instance, likened the concerto to caterwauling.

The Fourth String Quartet came about as a result of another commission from Elizabeth Sprague Coolidge. Although Schoenberg
could not have known that it would be his last quartet, the work is
so complete and so firmly anchored in the four-movement classical
tradition that he seems to be aiming to produce a quartet that
would be the summation of his work in this genre. It opens with
a clear theme-and-accompaniment statement, twelve-note, but it
is constructed according to a classical period and phrase structure.
These and similar vestiges of tonal procedures in the twelve-note
idiom later fuelled Pierre Boulez's impetuous dismissal of the late
Schoenberg as historically superseded, a criticism that unjustly
ignored the quartet's tremendous emotional power and structural
mastery. It is true that it looks back, but only obliquely, towards
Schoenberg's First and Second String Quartets, and to Beethoven's
late quartets. Even the human voice, the great novelty of the Second
Quartet, is hinted at in the long unison of all four instruments that
opens the third movement. The instrumental melody suggests
a vocal line straining to break into articulated utterance, only to dissolve
into individual contrapuntal strands. The striving to communicate

that is suggested by this third movement may reflect the struggle between the expression of a pure idea and the corruption of that idea through concrete images, a struggle that forms the dramatic and philosophical backbone of *Moses und Aron*. At the end of the opera's second act, where the unfinished work breaks off, Moses (a speaking role) says: 'O word, o word that I lack.' The third movement of the quartet is a wordless version of this struggle, alluding perhaps to Schoenberg's long-held belief in the superiority of music and its idea over the concreteness of the word.

Recreating a European spirit in the arts: Schoenberg against an Expressionist background (a portrait by Florence Homolka, the wife of the actor Oscar Homolka, whom Schoenberg knew in his Berlin days).

The Violin Concerto and the Fourth String Quartet were the first two compositions that Schoenberg completed in California, where he and the family had moved in September 1934 after leaving New York: they went first, briefly, to Pasadena and then to Hollywood. His teaching at the University of Southern California brought him the same problems and disappointments that he had encountered at the Malkin Conservatoire. The gap between his expectations and the students' abilities was simply too great, and the pedagogical and social conventions that he encountered were alien to him. In March 1935 he complained to his old friend David Josef Bach: 'Here everything is supposed to be praised: *marvelous, very nice, beautiful* ... But here, where everything is *all wrong*, it is the insecurity and fear of exposure that will only tolerate praise.' One of the hallmarks of Schoenberg's teaching lay in his challenging his pupils always to question and search, but many of his students still needed instruction in elementary harmony and counterpoint. This, he found, applied even to John Cage, who was already making a name as an experimental composer. The proximity of Hollywood also meant that some of those who wished to study with him rather naively hoped just to learn a trick or two which they could then apply to film scores – only to find that Schoenberg demanded from them a degree of dedication that deflected them from their imagined road to success.

The situation improved somewhat when, after a year, he moved to the more prestigious and bigger University of California in Los Angeles (UCLA), where he remained for the next nine years. Here he built up a class that included many young people whom he was able to inspire – even though they had to learn to take the rough with the smooth, often enduring Schoenberg's sarcasm and merciless criticism of their work. Dika Newlin, a child prodigy who joined his class in December 1938 aged only fourteen, provided in her diary a vivid account of a man who in quick succession could be protective, humorous, gloomy, childishly skittish, witty and devastatingly cruel. But from all these contrasts there emerge two dominant qualities: Schoenberg's unselfish devotion to his students and his real joy in communicating. The textbooks that he prepared for his students, *Preliminary Exercises in Counterpoint*, *Structural Functions of Harmony* and *Fundamentals of Musical Composition*, eventually became classics of their kind, especially in the English-speaking world.

John Cage, one of
Schoenberg's pupils, was
inspired by his teacher's
example to seek a new
way for music.

Two other, far more ambitious theoretical projects, which he had
begun in the 1920s and worked on sporadically in America, were
collections of penetrating analytical, critical and theoretical studies;
these, however, remained fragmentary and were not published until
almost half a century after Schoenberg's death.

The California and Los Angeles of the early 1930s were very
different from the way they are today, and, apart from the hub of
Hollywood, they seemed provincial in comparison with the East
Coast. But opportunities were there and the relatively low cost of
living attracted such a great number of refugees from Nazism and
racial persecution that by the late 1930s the world around Schoenberg
had become a Central Europe in miniature. Although this lent a
new vibrancy to various artistic activities, it also meant that the old
Central European resentments and animosities were transplanted

A harmony lecture at UCLA, 1940. Throughout his teaching career Schoenberg insisted on a thorough mastery of traditional harmony and counterpoint.

to the new surroundings. Otto Klemperer was already there when Schoenberg arrived, and by 1942 European exiles included, among others, Igor Stravinsky, Darius Milhaud, Thomas Mann, Bertolt Brecht, Hanns Eisler, Theodor Wiesengrund Adorno, Alma Mahler-Werfel, Franz Werfel and Erich Wolfgang Korngold.

The relationship between Schoenberg and Klemperer was as uneasy in California as it had been in Berlin. Schoenberg continued to resent Klemperer's reluctance to conduct his music, while

Klemperer (although he stuck to his guns as far as conducting
was concerned) came at one point to study musical analysis with
Schoenberg. Stravinsky and Schoenberg, in spite of living not
far from each other, were never in communication, and even their
mutual friends and acquaintances avoided mentioning one man's
name to the other. In contrast, Schoenberg's friendship with Eisler,
which had cooled considerably in the late 1920s, regained some of its
original warmth. Alma, as ever, remained both friendly and manipulative, and Schoenberg's friendship with Milhaud continued as
before. Relations with Thomas Mann began on the level of a distant
and formal cordiality but were to deteriorate after World War II.

A particular closeness developed between Schoenberg and George
Gershwin, giving the lie to the widespread belief that Schoenberg was
an élitist with no interest in popular culture. What he admired in the
Strauss brothers as much as in Franz Lehár and now in Gershwin
was their total command of the expressive and technical means in their
own genres. Gershwin, who had come into contact with Schoenberg's
music in Berlin in 1928, became fascinated with the composer both as
a man and as a musician. Gershwin moved to California in the
summer of 1936 and during the remaining year of his life a real
friendship between the composers developed, reinforced by a shared
interest in painting and tennis. Gershwin even expressed the wish
to study with him but Schoenberg dissuaded him, doubting that
a composer as confident in his chosen manner as Gershwin would
in any way benefit from his teaching. When Gershwin died, aged
only thirty-nine, Schoenberg was deeply affected, and on 12 July 1937
he recorded a moving tribute to his friend:

*George Gershwin was one of these rare kind of musicians to whom
music is not a matter of more or less ability. Music, to him, was the air
he breathed, the food which nourished him, the drink that refreshed him.
Music was what made him feel and music was the feeling he expressed.
Directness of this kind is given only to great men. And there is no doubt
that he was a great composer. What he has achieved was not only to the
benefit of a national American music but also a contribution to the
music of the whole world. In this meaning I want to express the deepest
grief for the deplorable loss to music. But may I mention that I lose also
a friend whose amiable personality was very dear to me.*

George Gershwin,
painting a portrait of
Schoenberg, autumn 1936.
On Gershwin's death in July
1937, Schoenberg recorded
a moving tribute, praising
the greatness of Gershwin's
achievements.

Schoenberg's letters of the late 1930s reveal an anxiety about friends
and family that is typical of an exile who bears the burden of guilt
towards those left behind. He had to be careful in his contacts with
Germany, and when Franz Schreker died he sent his widow a message of condolence on an open postcard without signing it. Berg's
letters from autumn 1935 made several references to performances
of Schoenberg's music in Vienna. On 30 November he wrote to
Schoenberg that a performance of the *Gurrelieder*, conducted by
Bruno Walter, had been enthusiastically applauded even by the
Austrian Vice-Chancellor, Prince Starhemberg. There was suddenly
something curious in the atmosphere of Vienna, with the Fascist-
inspired right-wing government now stressing the separateness of
Austria. Even Karl Kraus was willing to lend the government his
support in the hope of keeping Austria out of Hitler's clutches.
Starhemberg, probably overwhelmed by the impact of Schoenberg's

music, may have momentarily forgotten that both the composer and the conductor were Jewish; only fourteen years earlier, those inspired by Starhemberg had hounded the Jew Schoenberg out of Mattsee.

Berg's letter of 30 November would be the last he wrote to his teacher, for he died on 24 December and the news shook Schoenberg profoundly. He immediately told Berg's widow Helene that he would

Schoenberg with Charlie Chaplin, c. 1935. Schoenberg regularly watched Chaplin's films in his Berlin years.

complete the orchestration of the third act of Berg's opera *Lulu*, but when the score reached him he decided he could not do it. He explained to Erwin Stein that the characterization of the Jewish banker Puntschu in Franz Wedekind's play *Pandora's Box*, taken over by Berg as the basis for *Lulu*, made it impossible for him to engage with Berg's work. Adorno offered an uncharitable explanation of this decision, claiming that Schoenberg was too jealous of Berg's success as a musical dramatist and did not want to see *Lulu* ready for performance. Although some envy of Berg's success as an opera composer may have existed in Schoenberg's mind, Adorno possibly overstated his case.

During the early years of their regime the Nazis were willing to let Jews emigrate and even to take their possessions with them. So in 1936 Schoenberg could still draw the remaining amount of his Berlin salary. But since the money had to be spent in Germany, all he could do was to order books from German publishers. Schoenberg's furniture finally arrived from Berlin and went straight to the house in Brentwood Park, which he bought at the end of April. If he found the cultural climate of America deficient in many respects, he was at least able to enjoy some of the economic advantages that existed there – at the age of sixty-two he became a property owner for the very first time. In May 1936 a son, Rudolf Ronald, was born to the Schoenbergs and another son, Lawrence Adam, arrived in January 1941. The not-so-young father, whom the public knew from photographs and concert podiums as stern and intense, was a dedicated parent, fostering his children's talents and inventing entertaining games. He also managed to transmit to them his love of tennis and he devised a special shorthand in which to record the progress of a tennis game. (Ronald would eventually become a member of the US junior Davis Cup team.) Schoenberg's interest in and dependence on numerology and astrology played a part in the naming of both sons. The older boy's first name was that of his uncle Rudolf Kolisch, while his second name was an anagram of Arnold; the two names together contained twelve letters. The name Arnold for the younger boy was apparently ruled out by their friend, the astrologer Charlotte Dieterle, but she found the name Adam acceptable, and when paired with Lawrence, the two names again added up to the numerologically satisfactory twelve letters. For Schoenberg, numerology was not

Opposite, the Schoenberg family, summer 1941: Nuria in front of her father, next to her Ronald and Gertrud is holding Lawrence (born in January).

a superstition but a sincere belief, and in 1939 he even tried to interest Albert Einstein in the astrological work of his old friend Oskar Adler, which, predictably, Einstein dismissed as unscientific.

Schoenberg's dedication to and joy in his second family may have provided belated fulfilment of unrealized hopes from his first marriage. His daughter Trudi and son Georg (Görgi) had been growing up at a time when he was totally absorbed in his work, and he certainly never established a satisfactory relationship with his eldest son. Moreover, whatever hopes he may have had for Görgi becoming a musician were left unrealized as Görgi found the pressure of his father's expectations too much to bear and he struggled from one precarious job to another, with football as his only real interest. After the Anschluss, Görgi remained in Austria and managed to survive the war. Trudi and Felix Greissle succeeded in escaping to the United States, where Greissle became a senior editor at Schirmer. Although the relationship between father and daughter improved considerably during the exile years, the Greissle family nursed the suspicion that Schoenberg had not done enough to help Görgi to emigrate. Schoenberg's sister Ottilie Blumauer also survived the Holocaust and would outlive Schoenberg, but their younger brother Heinrich died in 1940 under suspicious circumstances in a Salzburg hospital, possibly as a victim of the Nazi euthanasia programme.

Webern's failure to take a clear stand against the Nazi regime became a source of concern for Schoenberg. It was clear where Berg had stood on this subject (although Schoenberg never quite believed it) and his early death spared him the difficulties that would have arisen for him after the Anschluss. But Webern was always so absorbed by his work that he walled himself up in a private world, displaying at times a staggering ignorance of what the new situation was bringing. First Louis Krasner, who had visited Webern, and then Eduard Steuermann and Fritz Stiedry, recently arrived in America as refugees, voiced their concerns about Webern's attitude to the Nazis and Schoenberg grew uneasy. In January 1937 he asked Webern pointedly whether he was a member of, or a sympathizer with the Nazi party and his friend denied it a little inconclusively, adding a rather evasive comment in the form of a question: 'Who dares to come between you and me?' While Webern's devotion to Schoenberg remained as sincere as ever, he seemed to think that

The pianist Leopold Godowsky, Albert Einstein and Schoenberg at a fundraising concert for Jewish refugees in Carnegie Hall, New York, April 1934.

an accommodation with the Nazis was possible. Only a few months after Schoenberg's question, Webern told the pianist Peter Stadlen, then preparing the first performance of Webern's Variations, Op. 27: 'If the Nazis come, I will go to Goebbels and tell him that he has been wrongly advised and that twelve-note music is no Cultural Bolshevism.' Stadlen's answer was that, even if he were to convince Goebbels of that, he would never convince him that Schoenberg was not a Jew. 'No, but in spite of that, he is a decent man,' was Webern's reply. Stadlen gave Webern the benefit of the doubt, interpreting 'in spite of' as referring to the Nazi attitude towards the Jews, while Steuermann was less sure about it. At the time, Webern was not aware that since 1935 his own name had figured in a list of 'Cultural Bolshevists' drawn up by the NS Amt für Kunstpflege (Nazi Office for the Fostering of Artistic Activity). Webern's music could no longer be performed in Austria after the Anschluss of March 1938, but in 1940, after World War II had started, the composer was expressing his enthusiasm for the recent German victories and wrote approvingly of Hitler's *Mein Kampf.*

The Nazi exhibition of *Entartete Musik* ('Degenerate Music'), which opened in Düsseldorf in May 1938, was like the previous one of 'Degenerate Art' in Munich in 1937, particularly explicit in branding the Jews as the chief carriers of all the alleged ills of Modernism. Apart from the obvious Jewish composers, such as Schoenberg, Weill, Korngold and Milhaud, the exhibition pilloried many others, including the 'Aryans' Hindemith, Berg, Webern and Stravinsky. The ground was being prepared for a much more radical onslaught on the Jewish community and the full wrath of the Nazis was finally unleashed on the *Kristallnacht* ('Crystal Night'), of 9–10 November 1938.

Opposite, title page of the catalogue for the *Entartete Musik* ('Degenerate Music') exhibition in Düsseldorf, May 1938. Ludwig Tersch's design parodies the poster for Ernst Krenek's opera *Jonny spielt auf* and features ritual objects of Nazi hatred: an 'inferior' black man, wearing the star of David and playing 'degenerate' jazz.

A little earlier, in July 1938, Schoenberg had written to Jakob Klatzkin in Switzerland: 'Composing is something I haven't done for two years. I have had too much other work. And anyway: whom should one write for?' In fact, in 1937 he had orchestrated Brahms's G minor Piano Quartet, but probably did not consider this task worthy of being called composing. The 'other work' that he mentioned was not just his teaching but also his actions on behalf of colleagues and friends who were seeking ways of coming to the United States and, once there, looking for work. Schoenberg's question of whom

to compose for was a reaction to the difficulties surrounding the reception of his music in America. This uncertainty is completely out of character, since Schoenberg always maintained that he was not composing in order to please an audience but in response to a deep urge. It is, however, an understandable appearance of doubt, since his music's expressive force was a sublimation of the cultural and psychological web provided by the intellectual and artistic tradition of German Modernism. Such a basis was lacking in America and Schoenberg's uncertainty was shared by many fellow-émigrés. Another Viennese exile, the writer Stefan Zweig, was affected particularly deeply by the feeling that a vital link with the German language was being denied him. But Schoenberg had always been a fighter and he avoided the depths of despair that drove Zweig, the poet Ernst Toller and several other Jewish exiles to suicide.

Schoenberg's examination of his position also reflected a quandary in which he found himself: would he now be expected to write 'Jewish' music that corresponded to the predominantly conservative tastes of his Jewish audience? He also voiced his concern that in Palestine there was a drive towards 'an authentically Jewish kind of music', something which, in spite of his own deeply felt Judaism and his belief in the necessity of a Jewish homeland, struck him as cultural provincialism. After all, while his most ambitious project, the opera *Moses und Aron*, was based on a Jewish subject, it involved universal questions about the meaning of existence and the nature of feelings and ideas in relation to the limitations of language. Interestingly, at about the time of his letter to Klatzkin, he received a request from Rabbi Jakob Sonderling to set the Sephardic lament 'Kol Nidre' to music. Sceptical at first, Schoenberg was won over by the explanation that the lament had originated in Spain at the time of the forcible conversion and expulsion of the Jews. By coincidence, the first performance, on 4 October 1938, came as a grim herald of *Kristallnacht* five weeks later. Schoenberg composed his *Kol Nidre* in a tonal idiom but refrained from any 'quaintness' that another composer might have been tempted to derive from the inflections of the Sephardic chant. Indeed, he said that he wanted to avoid the sentimentality that characterized Max Bruch's well-known version for cello and orchestra. Schoenberg's orchestral accompaniment to *Kol Nidre* has a gestural, dramatic character –

it sounds as if it is intended for a stage production or film. It is regrettable that Schoenberg wrote no film music while in California, or at least nothing beyond some sketches in response to an approach from MGM: the studio wanted to commission the music for the film *The Good Earth*, based on the popular novel by Pearl S. Buck. Schoenberg initially agreed but, wishing to preserve his artistic integrity, demanded that nothing in his music be changed and, according to Gertrud, set his fee impossibly high in the certain knowledge that it would not be acceptable. This provided Schoenberg with a way out, although he had denied himself a good source of income in the process. He was simply uncomfortable in any marketplace, unlike several of his fellow exiles, particularly Korngold.

Schoenberg's compositional output between 1939 and 1941 was small. The shock of the Anschluss and then the outbreak of war in Europe caused him great anxiety, which, in addition to the demands of teaching and his worsening health, sapped too much of his energy. Although there may have been pragmatic reasons behind his return to the long-abandoned Second Chamber Symphony, his decision to complete a work whose roots lay in the early part of the century suggests a desire to evoke the cultural and linguistic environment he had left behind. Between August and October 1939 he completed the first movement and added a second. The return to his earlier musical language was not easy, and this is reflected in the lack of drive that the Second Chamber Symphony shows when compared with its predecessor.

The war, which was closely monitored by the refugee community, was initially a distant affair in Europe for most Americans. It became a reality for the USA after Pearl Harbor, and especially so in California, since in December 1941, a few days after the USA entered the war, Japanese submarines became active off the coast there. In March 1942 Schoenberg received a commission (though without a fee) for a work celebrating the twentieth anniversary of the League of Composers, and the resulting composition, a setting of Byron's 'Ode to Napoleon', had a topical theme without being overtly propagandistic. Byron's condemnation of tyranny is set out in a series of images dealing with the misuse of power which, Schoenberg recognized, could equally well apply to Hitler. Byron's republican sympathies surface in the concluding stanza:

Where may the wearied eye repose
When gazing on the Great;
Where neither guilty glory glows,
Nor despicable state?
Yes – one – the first – the last – the best –
The Cincinnatus of the West,
Whom envy dared not hate,
Bequeath'd the name of Washington,
To make man blush there was but one!

This was not a sentiment that particularly attracted Schoenberg and in May 1942 he wrote to his daughter Trudi: 'The conclusion – to me surprising – is an homage to Washington.' He set Byron's poem for a reciter, but in a less elaborate manner than in *Pierrot lunaire*, with notes distributed above and below a one-line stave. The work is atonal, but does tend towards the key of E flat, a clear reference to Beethoven's *Eroica*, and Leonard Stein, who had helped Schoenberg to find a suitable text, claimed that the vocal inflections were meant to recall Winston Churchill's delivery. (Some years later Schoenberg was enraged when the work was performed with a female reciter.) Since the *Ode to Napoleon* had to wait for its first performance until November 1944, when Allied supremacy was indisputable, its dramatic impact was weaker than it would have been in the dark days of 1942.

Work on the *Ode* seemed to spur Schoenberg on to more composing, and he reacted enthusiastically to a suggestion by the pianist Oscar Levant that he write a concerto. But Levant could not pay the commission fee, so Schoenberg dedicated the work to Henry Shriver, a wealthy patron of the arts; nevertheless it was again the faithful Steuermann who gave the first performance. The four movements of the Piano Concerto, Op. 42, are rolled into a continuous whole, with reminiscences of the earlier material in the final movement – it was a new version of the formal model that he had used in his early works. Schoenberg's usual contrapuntally complex piano textures were dropped in favour of more percussive ones that were better suited to the interaction between the soloist and the orchestra. This, like the Violin Concerto, is another of the twentieth century's great works of its genre but, in welcome contrast, the first reactions to this new piece were different: the composer and critic Virgil Thomson reviewed it enthusiastically. The fact that later commentators claimed to have recognized in it textures ranging from the Viennese waltz via *Moses und Aron* to Gershwin indicates that the work is richly rewarding, and only the irrational fear of Schoenberg as being 'difficult' has prevented his Piano Concerto from becoming as well known as Bartók's or Prokofiev's concertos.

Schoenberg was only too aware of the aura of difficulty surrounding his work and tried to combat this prejudice not by making compromises and 'toning down' the works which he considered to be in his own mainstream, but by writing compositions which use the framework of tonality and so provide college ensembles with technically less demanding music. In the event, Schoenberg's music still turned out to be too demanding in comparison with that of such American composers as Aaron Copland, Roy Harris and William Schuman, all of whom were used to being more accommodating when writing for popular consumption. When Schoenberg encountered the same problem with the Variations for Wind Band, Op. 43, a piece that he wrote immediately after the Piano Concerto, he attempted to salvage the work by making a version of it for symphony orchestra (Op. 43b). His more sophisticated listeners,

Schoenberg surrounded by colleagues and students at his 65th birthday party, 13 September 1939.

unsurprisingly, found it less interesting: 'I hear a distantly romantic work with its predetermined harmonies,' commented the playwright and poet Bertolt Brecht.

In 1944 the tenth anniversary of Schoenberg's arrival in California coincided with his seventieth birthday and the rules of the University of California now applied: he had to retire, and his pension, based on his ten-year service, was to be $28.50 per month. He and his large family required something more than this derisory sum, but no exception was made by the university and he was now back where he had been in his Viennese days, forced to undertake private teaching and occasional lecturing, but now with his energy severely diminished by ill health. He was not able to thank all his well-wishers personally for their birthday greetings and had to do so by a circular letter. Towards its end there are a couple of lines which come from the heart of a dejected man: 'Many people wish me: "Many happy returns". Thank you, but how will that help?'

9

Schoenberg in the late 1940s.

You complain of lack of culture in this amusement-arcade world. I wonder what you'd say to the world in which I nearly die of disgust.

Schoenberg to Oskar Kokoschka,
3 July 1946

A Survivor from Europe 1944-51

In 1934, soon after his arrival in Los Angeles, Schoenberg had spoken at a reception. Being aware that his audience expected him to say something about the situation he had left behind in Germany, he apologized for having to disappoint them: he had come to the United States to escape from terror, not to speak about it – he was now 'driven into paradise'. In public Schoenberg tended to play down the difficulties he faced in America, claiming that the lack of understanding towards him resulted from cultural differences and naive ignorance but not from malice. However, the feeling that he could not easily fit into his environment never left him, and Schoenberg's true emotions – his sense of resignation and his disgust with consumer culture – came out in private and were reserved for friends and family: Zemlinsky during the brief period between his arrival in the United States in 1938 and his death in 1942, the Greissles in New York, Kokoschka, and Kolisch.

In photographs the smiles are evident when Schoenberg is surrounded by his children; otherwise the lens tellingly captures his increasingly gaunt face, deep-set eyes, and shrinking body in badly fitting clothes. In October 1944 Brecht was struck by the astonishing temperament within the 'Gandhi-like' frame and, although many other visitors at the time had the same impression of liveliness and nervous energy, Schoenberg was in fact not physically able to sustain other people's expectations and his own ambitions. He was supplementing his paltry pension with various activities, but invitations to attend performances and give lectures often had to be cancelled because of ill health. Diabetes and a heart condition – on top of his asthma – weakened him even further. His eyesight, too, had been deteriorating for some time. In 1942, soon after finishing the *Ode to Napoleon*, he had complained to Fritz Stiedry that he found it difficult to use manuscript paper with normal staves, and during the last few years of his life he had to use special paper with very wide staves. Never one to be deterred by lacking a tool needed for a specific purpose, he made for himself a rastrum, a holder with five aligned pencils, which enabled him to draw his own manuscript paper. For many years he had been the enthusiastic user of a typewriter, but as he could no longer cope with the normal typeface, his former pupil Paul Dessau, now working in Hollywood, presented him in spring 1946 with a typewriter with large letters, designed for use in film sets when a text had to be read at a distance.

Schoenberg's retirement from university teaching removed the attraction that California had previously had for him, and in October 1944 he even contemplated moving to New Zealand once the war was over. Hoping that there his American income would stretch further, he wrote an exploratory letter to his wife's uncle, Richard Hoffmann, who lived in New Zealand. This was a sign of deep despair, similar to what he must have felt when he believed that he could earn a living as a portrait painter. But he did not pursue the idea of the move, and he next attempted to improve his financial position by applying to the Guggenheim Foundation for a grant that would have enabled him to complete the *Jakobsleiter*, *Moses und Aron* and three theoretical works. He was refused. True, the foundation's rules stipulated that the recipient should be aged under thirty, although exceptions were allowed at the discretion of the Committee of Selection. Only a pedant with no interest in art would have considered this inflexible adherence to rules to be a sign of the committee's impartiality and propriety. Rather, this refusal is remembered as one of the more embarrassing episodes in the history of modern American culture.

Whether Schoenberg would have been able to complete the unfinished oratorio and opera is a different matter. The obstacles were not simply the state of his health and his financial position. The opera, and to a lesser extent the oratorio, were burdened by his determination to give them a philosophical import for which the music was to be the vehicle. This made the task of composition an act of unbearable responsibility which then turned into a deterrent. Arguably, in the two extant acts of *Moses und Aron* he had achieved all that the work needed to express and this may explain his inability to arrive at a satisfactory version of the text for the third act, in spite of many attempts at rewriting it. Schoenberg's sketches for the incomplete *Jakobsleiter*, however, contained enough substance and, even if

A retired professor, now teaching at home, c. 1948. In front of Schoenberg are Natalie Limonick, H. Endicott Hansen and Alfred Carlson. Schoenberg's failing eyesight forced him to use large sheets of manuscript paper, visible here on the board to his left.

Karl Rankl had to give up his attempt at completing them, in 1961 Winfried Zillig succeeded in accomplishing the task.

In the last few years of his life Schoenberg turned to works of a more compact nature, most of which were initiated by commissions. In the spring of 1946 the Music Department of Harvard University asked him for a work to be performed during a symposium on music criticism, so in June he sketched a twelve-note series for a String Trio for violin, viola and cello and worked on it until August, when a heart attack almost killed him. He was revived only by the rather risky intervention of a doctor who gave him an adrenalin injection directly into the heart muscle; subsequently Schoenberg claimed he had undergone an out-of-body experience, a conscious moment of hovering between life and death. But he resumed work on the Trio soon afterwards and completed it with a surprising speed and ease considering his health and the complexity of the score.

In October 1946 he told Thomas Mann that his agony was enshrined
in the very fabric of the Trio, and, indeed, twice in the composition
the violin plays a distorted version of the phrase to which, in the
final movement of his Second String Quartet, the voice sings Stefan
George's words 'Ich fühle Luft von anderem Planeten' – as if suggesting a glimpse of another world.

Although by no means a programmatic work, the Trio has that
same quality of immediacy that Schoenberg's Expressionist works
had had, and the discontinuities of its compact gestures are perhaps
the musical embodiments of a state of considerable tension. The Trio
also reverts to Schoenberg's one-movement form within which several
'Parts' and 'Episodes' (as he labelled them) produce an arch-like sym-
metrical design. The work achieves an amazing unity of opposites:
nervous, jagged moments are interspersed with lyrical passages, sudden
bursts of energy ebb away equally suddenly, and a variety of special
bowing techniques and harmonics combine with the normal sound
production. The serial technique that he employed here involves
a complex process of segmentation of the original row and the permutations of the segmented units of two, three or four notes.
These procedures, which can be found in Webern's music too, were
subsequently developed by the serial composers becoming prominent during the 1950s, particularly Pierre Boulez and Luigi Nono
in Europe and Milton Babbitt in the USA. Schoenberg felt that
the Trio was his best work, and it does indeed occupy a very special
place in his output since it captures so much of what he wanted to
achieve: expression and immediacy, a sound-world of remarkable
uniqueness, and a deep logic underpinning the whole structure.
All these were the principles that had intrigued him since his first
attempts at twelve-note composition in the early 1920s.

When, in July 1947, the Koussevitzky Foundation approached
Schoenberg with a commission for a new work, he revived the idea
that had first arisen when the choreographer Corinne Chochem
suggested to him a piece commemorating the suffering of the Jews
in Poland. Schoenberg wrote the text for *A Survivor from Warsaw*
himself. The piece is a short and disturbing account of one of the
many episodes of Nazi cruelty and the despair of their Jewish victims,
ending with the prayer 'Shema Yisroel', which adds defiance and
a ray of hope to the prevailing gloom. Schoenberg once again had

recourse to the semi-spoken voice for the narrator and created a shattering emotional effect through the interaction of the narrator, chorus and orchestra in a work that lasts barely nine minutes. This piece remains one of the most potent commemorations of the victims of the Holocaust, a chilling musical portrayal of terror by the man who, thirteen years earlier, had said that he did not want to speak about the terror, but who now felt compelled to do so, having seen his worst fears of anti-Semitism played out on a vast European scale. While Schoenberg's large-scale manuscript paper was suitable for sketching, it was of no use for compiling full scores and the score of *A Survivor from Warsaw* had to be copied in its final form by René Leibowitz, a young French composer who emerged as a persistent advocate of twelve-note music in post-war Europe.

Health and physical disability, rather than a lack of ideas, were thus the main reasons why Schoenberg's creative power waned, and during the remaining three years of his life he managed to complete only four compositions. In 1948 he produced new versions of three folksong texts that he had first set to music in 1932, and in 1949 there followed the Phantasy for Violin with Piano Accompaniment, Op. 47. Schoenberg deliberately chose this wording in order to indicate the process of composition: determined to ensure the unbroken flow of the violin part, he composed it first, adding the piano accompaniment afterwards. Immediately after this work, and as if wishing to sum up his emotions and beliefs towards the very end of his life, Schoenberg returned to the *a cappella* choral textures reminiscent of *Friede auf Erden*. A few days before the proclamation of the state of Israel on 15 May 1949, he wrote an *a cappella* setting of Dagobert Runes's *Dreimal tausend Jahre*, a poem expressing the symbolic Jewish longing for a return to Jerusalem. This he intended to follow with *Israel Exists Again*, for choir and orchestra, but it remained a fragment consisting of fifty-five bars.

In June and July 1950, another *a cappella* setting came in response to a request from an old Berlin acquaintance, the conductor Chemjo Vinaver, who was putting together an anthology of Jewish music. For this, Schoenberg turned to Psalm 130 and gave it its Latin title, *De profundis*, even though he actually set the Hebrew text 'Shir hama'alot mima'amakim'. There is something monumentally sublime in this deeply felt setting. Klemperer had once criticized Schoenberg's lack

A page of the manuscript of the String Trio, Op. 45 (1946), written on extra-large staves, drawn on two sheets of outsized manuscript paper taped together.

Ruins, and not a survivor
in sight: Warsaw in 1944.
Schoenberg's *A Survivor
from Warsaw*, composed in
1947, is one of the most
potent commemorations of
the victims of the Holocaust.

of feeling for the stage, but this does not mean that he lacked the
ability to express the dramatic. Indeed, it could be said that the
standard requirements of the stage – space, movement and acting –
limited Schoenberg's innate ability to present the dramatic component of music through sound alone. In *De profundis* a striking effect
is achieved when the spoken syllables 'A-do-nai' are heard against
a held chord. The lyricism and the full sonorities again recall *Friede
auf Erden*, even though the Psalm and *Dreimal tausend Jahre* are
entirely governed by the twelve-note series. Schoenberg later dedicated the Psalm 'to the State of Israel', and yet it is not an occasional
piece. Psalm 130 is one of the penitential psalms and, although the

last two verses mention the people of Israel, the sentiment is a personal one – it is a prayer for the forgiveness of sins and serves as Schoenberg's valedictory statement. Towards the end of his life Schoenberg wrote the text for eighteen *Modern Psalms*, or, as he had originally called them, *Conversations with and about God*, but only fragmentary settings of two of these remain. The words 'And yet, I pray...' from one of them were the last that he set to music.

Schoenberg lived for six years after the end of World War II. Peace hardly meant a return to normality, for his financial situation was still precarious, and in a way it was the war years, when he could at least rely on a regular salary, that offered up a kind of normality. In these post-war years he also suffered greater personal grief, with the news of Webern's tragic death in autumn 1945 shaking him particularly deeply. Of course, there had been ups and downs in their relationship, but even if he was aware of his friend's inability to distance himself from the Nazis, Schoenberg saw Webern as the last remaining link with his early Viennese years, once Berg and Zemlinsky had died. And then, in October 1947, Schoenberg's daughter Trudi died in New York.

The world around him continued to offer a curious mixture of recognition and hostility. Musical life in Germany was gradually picking up, and the news of the first post-war performances of his works, after the Nazi blackout of some thirteen years, certainly brought encouragement. His staunch pre-war supporters, Winfried Zillig, Hermann Scherchen, Josef Rufer and Hans Rosbaud, were now joined in France by René Leibowitz, and in Italy Luigi Dallapiccola did much to advance the cause of the Viennese avant garde. Summer courses for new music began at Darmstadt, in the US-occupied sector of post-war West Germany in 1946 and became the focal point for the dissemination of new ideas. They also offered younger German composers the opportunity of catching up and filling in the vacuum created by the Nazis' cultural policies. But the tensions among the various stylistic camps during the 1920s and 1930s, which had been put to one side during the war, reappeared once normal communication was resumed between Europe and the United States, where many of the exiles had settled. Many axes were still ground assiduously. In America, outside the circle of sympathetic critics and composers who felt a community of purpose with Schoenberg (such as Roger Sessions, Virgil Thomson, Henry Cowell and John Cage), references

The Schoenbergs with Erika
Wagner (far right), c. 1948.
Lawrence is holding the
dog Laddie, his brother
Ronald is next to him, and
at the back (left to right),
Gertrud, Nuria and
Schoenberg. The photo was
taken by Fritz Stiedry, Erika
Wagner's husband.

to him were still accompanied by such labels as 'the wild man of music', 'the purveyor of dissonances', 'the composer who writes difficult music'. Difficulty and exclusivity were stressed and, in a society where market forces rather than aesthetic considerations had a crucial impact on the recording, performance and printing of music, Schoenberg felt that he was being assailed without being given a fair hearing. There was a degree of stubborn rejection of commercial pragmatism in everything Schoenberg did, and in 1950, in an interview with the *Los Angeles Times,* he reiterated his pride in his independence: 'Maybe I had four times four times [*sic*] harder to work for a living. But I made no concessions to the market.' One can surmise that here he was thinking less of Hollywood film composers and more of Stravinsky or Hindemith. Stravinsky was, indeed, an adroit manipulator of copyright laws, producing retouched versions of older works just as they were about to go out of copyright, and for Schoenberg, of course, he would forever remain the 'Modernsky' who knew how to exploit new stylistic trends. Schoenberg's rejection of Stravinsky had its roots in his old weakness that caused him to see various trends and tendencies around him as impinging upon him in some malevolent way. This was a bitter residue of his long years of confrontation with uncomprehending critics, and may go even further back, to the time when he had to claw his way upwards from the position of social and cultural outsider in a snobbish and intolerant Viennese society.

Schoenberg's feelings of rejection and his sense of the animosity towards him may have been exaggerated but they were by no means unfounded. The Darmstadt summer course seemed to be only an oasis in which twelve-note music found its spiritual home and, after a brief initial show of support for it, the Information Control Division (ICD) of the US Military Government in Germany became reluctant to support this forum for the avant garde. The ICD's reluctance extended to the promotion of the more radical avant-garde music in general, while favouring more approachable modern composers such as Shostakovich, Copland and Benjamin Britten. Quite understandably, the Military Government wanted to replace the exclusively German programme orientation of the Nazi period with a more cosmopolitan choice. In reality, their programmes failed to meet the expectations of older and younger audiences alike. Where the older members were

deprived of their standard classical fare, the younger ones, now becoming aware of the suppressed tendencies in pre-war music, were
disappointed by the lack of opportunity to hear this music performed.
Harrison Kerr, head of the music office of the ICD, instituted a
policy of promoting American music, ignoring requests from the
department's field officers to invite Hindemith and Schoenberg
for a visit. The emphasis remained on American composers and
performers even when, to the sophisticated German audience, they
appeared less good than those from Germany. Eventually, an invitation was extended to Hindemith in February 1949 as part of the
educational programme, since he held a chair of music theory at Yale.
In the 1940s Hindemith was in the process of retreating from his
earlier style, to the extent of toning down the dissonances in some
of his music from the 1920s. He used his lecture in the Great Hall
of Munich University to denounce twelve-note composition and
the composers of such music. This was a spiteful gesture on the
part of a composer who sensed that his brand of neo-classicism was
considered outdated by the younger German composers – they saw
him as having been too close to the type of music tolerated by the
Nazis, even though, in the 1930s, he had had his share of political
difficulties. Ironically, the previous condemnation of avant-garde
music coming from the same Great Hall had been in a speech given
by Alfred Heuss in March 1929 on behalf of the Kampfbund für
deutsche Kultur (Fighting League for German Culture).

But even if the American authorities had been better disposed
towards the idea of organizing Schoenberg's trip to Europe, it is
unlikely that he would have been able to travel. During the late
1940s his health forced him to decline other invitations to Europe.
For example, several gestures were made in Vienna to redress old
injustices. The first came as early as April 1946 when the Lord Mayor
invited Schoenberg to return and teach there. In 1949 the Austrian
Society of Dramatists and Composers made him an honorary
member on the occasion of his seventy-fifth birthday and as a
gesture of atonement for having rejected him for membership
in 1935. In his letter of thanks to the association he wrote: 'I myself
dearly wish that my health may permit me to come to Vienna, where
I still have – in intensity and perhaps even in number – friends so
many as to exceed the number of my opponents.' The culminating

official gesture came in September 1949 when he was awarded the
freedom of the city of Vienna. Schoenberg's old animosity towards
the ISCM, which had all the markings of his focusing on a real or
imagined enemy (in this particular case on E. J. Dent), was now a
thing of the past. Shortly after the ISCM resumed full activity after
the war, Schoenberg was elected Honorary President. News of the
last honour to be bestowed on him, the Presidency of the Israel
Academy of Music in Jerusalem, reached him in April 1951, three
months before his death. All this may suggest that towards the end
of his life he was content in the knowledge that his true stature was
finally being acknowledged in Europe. But for him the honours
and recognition that came from Vienna had more than a symbolic
significance: they finally vindicated him as a composer who had
stubbornly persisted in the pursuit of his creative ideas.

His Californian reality was different, though. A dark cloud
appeared in 1947 and continued to cast its shadow over Schoenberg
during the remaining years of his life. Towards the end of World
War II it became known among Thomas Mann's friends that he was
writing a new novel, whose protagonist was a contemporary composer.
When *Doktor Faustus. Das Leben des deutschen Tonkünstlers Adrian
Leverkühn, erzählt von einem Freunde* ('Doctor Faustus, the Life
of the German Composer Adrian Leverkühn as Told by a Friend')
was published in October 1947, it became apparent that, even if
Schoenberg were not himself Adrian Leverkühn, his twelve-note
music was the model for Leverkühn's innovative musical language.
But the novel is a depiction of alienation and the disintegration of
a personality: Leverkühn makes a Faustian pact with the Devil that
leads him to a syphilis-induced madness. Moreover, Leverkühn's life
and fate are intended as a symbolic representation of the disintegration of German culture during the Third Reich. In *Doktor Faustus*
Mann adopted the cinematic technique of 'assemblage' or 'montage' –
he constantly changes the novel's perspective, combining views that
come either directly from the narrator, Leverkühn's friend Serenus
Zeitblom, or indirectly from Leverkühn himself. The boundary between verifiable historical reality and novelistic imagination was
deliberately blurred by Mann's references to real personalities from
the musical world, and although Schoenberg is nowhere mentioned
by name, there are many pointers in his direction.

Schoenberg initially considered Mann a friend – although their first contact in 1930 through correspondence had already revealed the profound differences between the two great men. On that occasion Schoenberg had asked Mann to sign a petition in support of Adolf Loos but Mann declined, saying that he had never been interested in Loos's ideas or writings. Here he was being absolutely honest: he had very little understanding of modernity and modern art, since his spiritual world was that of the late Wilhelmine period and his heroes were Goethe and Wagner. Of Mann's attitude to music, the novelist Hermann Hesse offered this sharp observation in 1949: 'It is romantic and based on feelings, and with an immense amount of effort he has turned it into an intellectual one.'

Thomas Mann in his study in Pacific Palisades. Living close to each other, Mann and Schoenberg often met, but were estranged when Schoenberg took offence at Mann's portrayal of a Schoenberg-like character in his *Doktor Faustus*.

Schoenberg and Mann were now neighbours in California and each of them was keen to experience the other's ideas. However, Mann selfishly exploited Schoenberg as an instructor in general musical matters, while never telling him that he was writing a novel based on an interpretation of his music. Mann's depiction of Leverkühn's

compositional technique was closely based on information about Schoenberg's twelve-note music that had been provided by another California-based exile, Theodor Adorno. Adorno's enthusiasm for Schoenberg's Expressionist period was tempered by a scepticism about some aspects of serial technique, and his relationship with Schoenberg had never been easy. He now welcomed the chance to appear as Mann's 'secret adviser', as the novelist called him, even referring to him in the novel by his own original name, Wiesengrund.

Mann wrote *Doktor Faustus* between May 1943 and January 1947 and during that time he and Schoenberg met often. In his diary Mann reports friendly conversations with Schoenberg, but other references clearly show his lack of understanding of or even interest in his music. He knew very little of Schoenberg's advanced music and found even *Verklärte Nacht* to be 'lacking in substance', 'formless' and 'too Tristan-like'. In March 1947, soon after completing the novel, the tone of Mann's diary entries changed and he recorded, with a hint of irritation, that Schoenberg was 'hanging around' him, always wanting to talk to him. It was as if Mann no longer had any use for him once

Theodor Adorno in California, early 1940s. Adorno was Schoenberg's advocate in public and a troubled admirer in private. He acted as Mann's 'secret adviser' during the writing of *Doktor Faustus*.

the novel was out of the way. (In February 1948, after listening to an excerpt from the final scene of Wagner's *Das Rheingold*, he noted: 'I would give for this piece all of Schoenberg's, Berg's and Krenek's music, and Leverkühn's too.')

When *Doktor Faustus* was published, Mann sent an inscribed copy to Schoenberg; as always, Mann was primarily absorbed in his own ideas and quite unaware of the effect the novel would have. Schoenberg was deeply offended by Mann's appropriation of his twelve-note method of composition without asking him for permission. But even more offensive to him than this form of plagiarism was Mann's portrayal of Schoenberg's achievement as an image of cultural decline. Mann later tried to deny that he had had Schoenberg in mind, even though the link had long been known in Mann's circle. As early as September 1943, Adorno had written to his parents that Mann was writing a novel in which 'the main character is based on Schoenberg in some way or another'.

Schoenberg's first response to Mann's novel was to pen a little literary fantasy in which Mann appears as the true inventor of the twelve-note method; Mann, however, was not able to see Schoenberg's point and dismissed the piece as an 'enraged attack'. Schoenberg then – unwisely – demanded that Mann insert in future editions a note acknowledging Schoenberg's invention of the twelve-note method. Mann took this as a sign of Schoenberg's small-mindedness and, in the note that he did insert, described Schoenberg merely as 'a contemporary composer', thus compounding his high-handedness. Schoenberg's impatience to protect what he felt was rightfully his had led him to concentrate on the acknowledgement of his authorship and to miss an opportunity to expose the basic weakness of Mann's novel: his lack of understanding of Modernist culture and his arrogance, that had led him to cast himself as its judge. A long polemic between them then ensued in private letters and in *The Saturday Review of Literature* and the *Music Survey*, and after the publication of *Doktor Faustus* they never spoke to one another again. When Schoenberg's seventy-fifth birthday was celebrated in America and Europe, Mann was not among the well-wishers. Indeed, following a conversation at a dinner party on the day after Schoenberg's birthday and the broadcast performance of the Phantasy for Violin with Piano Accompaniment, Op. 47, Mann wrote in his diary: 'Much against Schoenberg, whose music ought to be better in order to balance his foolishness.' This is a sad comment, not on Schoenberg but on Mann himself.

In January 1950 Schoenberg wrote to Mann with an offer to bury the hatchet, which Mann accepted, but a final reconciliation never took place. Mann and Schoenberg were in some respects too similar: each was immensely proud and each was convinced of his own importance. Schoenberg valued Mann as a great intellectual equal, and yet throughout this episode Mann exhibited all the faults of his character: self-importance and a patrician disdain for those around him whom he regarded as his inferiors. Franca Magnani, who knew Mann in Zurich in the 1930s, experienced this side of his character and recorded in her memoirs: 'My admiration towards him as a writer increased every time I read one of his books, as did my antipathy towards him as a man each time I encountered him.'

Thus, controversy and a feeling of persecution followed Schoenberg from his early days in Vienna to the very end of his life in California. The publication of Theodor Adorno's *The Philosophy of New Music*, in autumn 1949, also hurt him. Adorno's 'parallel lives' approach pitted Schoenberg the avant-gardist against Stravinsky the conservative, though Adorno's relatively mild criticism of some of the implications of Schoenberg's twelve-note principle – such as the danger of an excessive rationalization of music – was more than offset by the philosopher's merciless onslaught on Stravinsky as a bearer of retrogressive tendencies in contemporary music. By then Schoenberg was too distrustful of the world around him and too frail to engage in a new polemic. Moreover, his sight had become so weak that he could no longer read and this was a convenient excuse for not engaging with Adorno's book beyond listening to a few excerpts that were read to him. In his will Schoenberg specified that Adorno should be excluded from participating in the preparation of any of his manuscripts for posthumous publication.

IO

Schoenberg receiving the
certificate of the honorary
citizenship of Vienna, in the
interval of a concert held in
his honour in Los Angeles,
23 October 1949.

*The second half of this century will spoil by
overestimation all the good of me that the first
half, by underestimation, has left intact.*

Arnold Schoenberg in 1949,
quoting one of his earlier aphorisms

Schoenberg's Legacy

At the beginning of July 1951, the 'Dance round the Golden Calf'
from the third scene of the second act of *Moses und Aron* was given
its first performance by Hermann Scherchen in Darmstadt. During
the previous year some of Schoenberg's friends had still entertained
the hope that he might complete the opera, even though this was
quite an unrealistic expectation. For even if the final structure of the
text for the third act had been clear in his mind, Schoenberg was
now too much of an invalid to embark on the task of composition.
The enthusiastically received orchestral fragment therefore
remained as a symbol of unfulfilled aspirations – Schoenberg died
in Los Angeles eleven days later, on 13 July 1951.

Schoenberg's grandson Arnold Greissle-Schönberg reports the
occasion when Schoenberg as a young bank clerk was on his way
to his office and an old lady came up to him, grabbed his hand,
looked at it and said: 'You will have a difficult life, young man. The
number thirteen signifies bad luck for you. Beware particularly of
13 June or 13 July. Those are bad dates for you.' Schoenberg shared
the belief in numerology, in portents, symbols and the mystagogical
powers of certain individuals that was widespread not only in Vienna
but also among the Modernists in Central and Western Europe in
general. Of course, the number 13 is commonly associated with bad
luck and it is easy to see that Schoenberg, born on 13 September,
would have attached some considerable significance to the prophecy
of the itinerant clairvoyant; indeed, throughout his life he avoided
this number. Depending on one's attitude towards the significance
of numbers, it is either chance or a matter of profound symbolism
that Schoenberg died at 11.45 p.m. on 13 July, the date against which he
had been warned. A curious mistake occurred on the death certificate
that was issued by the Los Angeles Department of Public Health:
Schoenberg's date of birth, 13 September 1874, is erroneously recorded
as 'July 13, 1875'. A death mask, showing Schoenberg's emaciated bony
countenance, was made by the sculptress Anna Mahler, Gustav and

Alma's daughter, who had recently moved from London to Los Angeles.
This was an act of quasi-religious significance: a lasting record of a
lifeless, but by no means expressionless, Schoenberg was created by
the daughter of a man who, half a century earlier, had been among
the first to sense the force of the composer's creative talent. In 1974,
the centenary of Schoenberg's birth, the urn containing his ashes
was transferred to the Vienna Central Cemetery, together with that
of Gertrud Schoenberg, who died in 1967.

'Since the death of Arnold Schoenberg, Stravinsky is beyond any
doubt the greatest living composer,' Otto Klemperer stated in 1961.
Ten years later, Oskar Kokoschka wrote in his autobiography: 'To
me, Schönberg was one of the last remaining links with classical music,
late Schubert, Bruckner and Beethoven.' These judgements, one by
a fellow musician with a history of a difficult relationship with
Schoenberg, the other by a fellow fighter from the heady days of
European Modernism, seem to sum up the difficulty that audiences,
critics and historians alike had with Schoenberg both during his life
and after his death. Klemperer places Schoenberg in the context
of his time, Kokoschka invokes a historical backdrop against which
he judged his friend – but at the same time each man would have
endorsed the other's judgement. It was the breadth of Schoenberg's
vision and the range of his musical references that made him so
inspiring a teacher and so self-critical a composer. In addition, he
combined an intuitive approach to composition with an ability to
rationalize acts of intuition through references to a range of structural principles derived from past composers. Schoenberg is often
described as a 'conservative revolutionary', but the phrase does not
explain much. The term 'conservative' is highly misleading since
it suggests that Schoenberg was trying to preserve aspects of the
past intact. In fact, his aim was to keep the historical backdrop as
a point of reference, while devising a musical language in relation
to that backdrop whose aural impact would be highly individual
and new. Schoenberg's compositions require a conscious intellectual
effort on the part of the listener, and are as such the musical equiv-
alents of James Joyce's prose, in which complex syntax combines
with a range of allusions to literary topics from the past. Schoenberg
confronted his audiences with a comparable 'difficulty' quite early
on, and although the novel sound made him a man of his time,

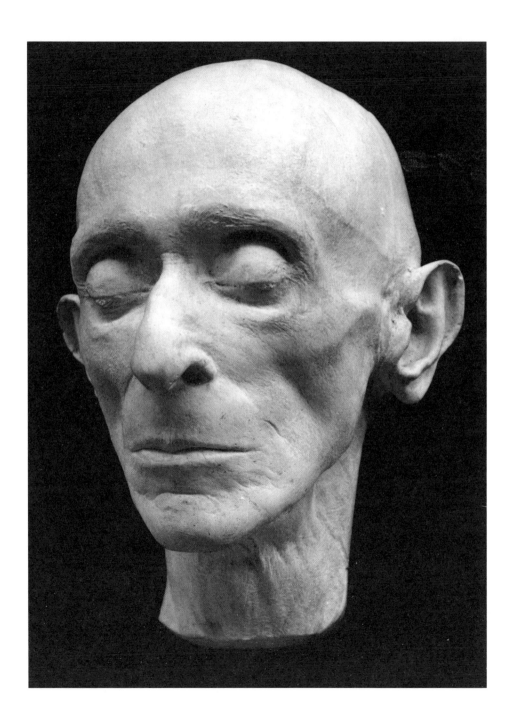

he was, equally, appealing to his audience's intuitive ability to hear his music against the great tradition of German music. Klemperer's and Kokoschka's comments identify the core of the 'Schoenberg problem': Bach's counterpoint, Mozart's motivic transformations, Beethoven's formal complexity and Brahms's ingenuity in large-scale planning all found their way into Schoenberg's 'modern' textures.

Schoenberg's own convictions about the worth of his music – and the way in which it should be listened to – involve an ambivalence, a contradiction that further complicates the 'Schoenberg problem'. On the one hand Schoenberg believed that the historical background which is an intellectual and technical component of his music needed to be both understood and felt in the process of listening. On the other hand, he repeatedly expressed the hope that his music would be listened to without preconceptions and, especially in the twelve-note works, without the aim of tracking down the notes of the series or row. He warned his brother-in-law Rudolf Kolisch against trying to identify the notes of the row in the Third String Quartet, and in a letter to Hans Keller he complained about those who 'look in my music only for the twelve notes – not realizing in the least its musical contents, expression and merits'. His conviction that his music should be listened to as music, rather than as a source of knowledge about technical properties, was a reasonable one. It was also true that a system so individual and so novel as twelve-note music, in the late 1920s and the early 1930s, would be bound to awaken curiosity about its technical features. Berg's and Webern's own versions of the twelve-note method were sure signs that his system was neither limited nor rigid. Webern favoured ascetic and sparse sound-structures based on meticulous handling of the series, while Berg sought ways of combining serialism with delicate hints of tonal procedures. But then a rupture occurred. The advent of Nazism stopped the activity of Schoenberg's, Berg's and Webern's German publishers; only very little of Schoenberg's later music was available in the USA, and none of it reached Europe in the late 1930s or during the war.

A poignant conclusion to a long association between Schoenberg and the family of Gustav Mahler: Schoenberg's death mask by Anna Mahler, daughter of Gustav and Alma Mahler.

When an interest in Schoenberg was reawakened in Europe at the end of the war, no major composer of twelve-note music was to be found in Germany, and in France only a few isolated individuals were familiar with his music. In these circumstances Schoenberg became detached from the cultural and psychological conditions that

had given rise to his innovation, and his music became an object of
dispassionate analysis. Nevertheless, the dispassionate nature of this
analysis led to passionate conclusions.

Nadia Boulanger (whom Adorno called 'Stravinsky's pedagogical
regent') held court in Paris as an opponent of the Viennese avant
garde, and so it is paradoxical that several composers in the French
capital took a serious interest in Schoenberg at the end of World
War II. René Leibowitz was an enthusiast, and his *Schönberg et son
école* ('Schoenberg and His School'), published in 1946, became the
first guide to Schoenberg's compositional methods, with the result
that the reception of Schoenberg was influenced primarily by a
rational examination of his serial procedure. This was contrary to
Leibowitz's intentions, for he had wanted to communicate his
enthusiasm for the music of the Vienna School with the analytical
aspect as his means and not an end in itself.

Nevertheless it seems that it was the fundamentally abstract principles of twelve-note structuring that appealed to Olivier Messiaen
and to his and Leibowitz's pupil Pierre Boulez – as though those
principles were a set of mathematical ideas. The French composers'
approach had all the characteristics of classical rationality and the
Parisian desire to appear intellectually tidy. Messiaen and Boulez
contended that if the melodic component of music was to be governed by a series of twelve notes, then this principle should be
extended to the organization of the music's rhythmic and dynamic
aspects. Messiaen started developing his thoughts along these lines
in 1946, and his remarkable *Mode de valeurs et d'intensités* was
performed at Darmstadt in 1949. In this piano piece the pitches,
rhythmic durations and modes of articulation are governed by
a series of twelve discrete 'values', while a series of seven 'intensities'
determine the dynamics.

Boulez, as well as Karlheinz Stockhausen, took this a stage further
by subjecting all the parameters of his music to a series of twelve.
The surface logic masked an illogical procedure, for while the pitches
conform to the necessary twelve chromatic notes of the Western
musical system, there is very little reason, other than a sleight of
hand, to force the series of twelve on the rhythm or dynamics. Here,
Schoenberg was hoisted by his own petard: if his determination
to extend the boundaries of expressive means and of principles of

construction was justified by an appeal to historical necessity, then Boulez felt justified in tidying up what he felt had been overlooked by Schoenberg. Boulez's essay that served as Schoenberg's obituary was entitled 'Schoenberg is Dead', and in it his 'Young Turk' zeal resembled Schoenberg's own eagerness to assert himself in the early years of the twentieth century. But Boulez expressed himself in strongly partisan terms that were characteristic of the post-1945 generation's desire to liberate itself from the burdens of the past. In spite of Boulez's provocative title, Schoenberg at least mattered to him: 'since the discoveries of the Viennese School, all non-serial composers are *useless*,' he asserted in the obituary, and some twenty years later Boulez the conductor emerged as one of the most consistent advocates of Schoenberg's music.

An unlikely convert to serial procedures was Igor Stravinsky. His distance from Schoenberg had been partly a response to Schoenberg's criticism, but after the opera *The Rake's Progress* (1951) he sensed the waning of the force of his own neo-classicism and adroitly adapted serial procedures to suit his own style. In this he was aided by Robert Craft, who admired both Schoenberg and Stravinsky and was determined to introduce Stravinsky to the twelve-note method.

'The Worship of the Golden Calf' – scene from a production of Moses *und Aron* at the Bavarian State Opera in Munich, June 2006.

There was something evasive in Stravinsky's claim that his model was Webern and not Schoenberg. Webern, of course, did emerge in the 1950s and 1960s as the chief mentor of the new generation of serial composers who, following Boulez, felt that in Webern they had found a purer application of serialism, devoid of the pseudo-tonal remnants that floated in Schoenberg's music. Nevertheless, Stravinsky's early serial works, especially *In memoriam Dylan Thomas*, owe much to Schoenberg.

Just as Boulez's obituary combined a tribute to Schoenberg with a serious criticism of his alleged weaknesses (primarily a reluctance to abandon rhythmic models redolent of tonal music), young composers in the 1950s and 1960s were subjected to the conflicting experiences of being overwhelmed by the adulation of Schoenberg, Berg and Webern and of needing, understandably, to distance themselves from the ever-increasing complexities of Boulez's integrative method of 'total serialism'. In fact, several American composers had already been pursuing a path that was radically different from Schoenberg's musical logic, although the most influential of them, Schoenberg's admirer and one-time student John Cage, acted from the conviction that he was further extending his mentor's ideas. Schoenberg's emancipation of dissonance led, according to Cage, towards the emancipation of the sound itself; this in turn led Cage to the conviction that structural principles should not be imposed on material, which should be allowed to present itself in a succession of chance operations. Cage's, however, is an extreme case. Rather, it has been composers such as Luigi Nono in Italy and Peter Maxwell Davies, Harrison Birtwistle and Alexander Goehr in Britain who, each in his own way, have retained some aspects of serial structuring while not abandoning the sheer musical and dramatic excitement of the Expressionist Schoenberg. In the USA Milton Babbitt, in spite of his leanings towards a total serial control, retained his belief in Schoenberg's imaginative writing.

There is no doubt that the growing complexity and dissonant quality of much twentieth-century music alienated a wider audience, and the return in the 1960s to various forms of a 'new simplicity' (as in some of the minimalist works that display an insipid and mo-notonous euphony) only contributed to the perception that the 'new music' was experiencing a prolonged crisis. Unjustifiably, the blame for this is often laid at Schoenberg's door, and he is singled out as an originator of the alienation and dissolution that affects Modernism in general. This judgement disregards the enormous diversity of Modernism and the fact that, if anything, Schoenberg was one of those rare individuals able to sense the discontent of modern culture as evinced in the early phase of Modernism, especially in Central Europe, and to derive from this discontent powerful works that both embody and criticize the emotional and psychological tensions of Modernism. It is not surprising that the Expressionist and serial Schoenberg is now experiencing something of a resurgence in continental Europe, whereas in Britain and the USA, countries largely unaffected by the early Modernist movement, he is best known for his early *Verklärte Nacht* and the *Gurrelieder*, the works that celebrate the very Romantic narrativity from which he tried to distance himself in his later music.

By the end of the twentieth century Schoenberg the theorist was accepted by music critics and musicologists with less resistance than Schoenberg the composer was accepted by audiences. Yet as a theorist he was not a propagandist for his own musical cause but, possibly, the last great interpreter of the compositional theory of tonal music. In contrast, the theorist-composers of the subsequent fifty years invariably tried to advance only their own causes. Schoenberg believed that his music could make a sufficient plea on its own behalf, but some of the critical prejudices, first formed in the early years of the twentieth century, proved too tenacious. Interestingly, those rare critics such as Hans Keller, who insisted that Schoenberg's music should be listened to without prejudice and with understanding, succeeded in bringing Schoenberg closer to wider audiences.

Unlike Webern or Berg, Schoenberg continues to find himself in a vicious circle. Webern's star, having shot very high in the 1950s, has descended somewhat, since he was too closely associated with the excess of rationalization that affected Western music in the period after World War II. Berg, possibly the only one of the Viennese avant-gardists who had an instinctive feel for the stage, is now celebrated for his operas. Schoenberg, meanwhile, continues to perplex. His output is so varied and so far-reaching in its significance that more than half a century after his death many composers seem not to feel quite at ease until they have at least tried to define their own

aspirations in relation to the challenges that he posed. Once freed
from the belief (fostered by the commercial producers of recorded
sound) that music primarily provides a soothing background,
listeners will find that Schoenberg's music offers a combination of
aural richness and intellectual challenge comparable to the demands
placed upon them by Bach, Beethoven, Chopin or Debussy. In this
sense Schoenberg's comment that 'the second half of this century
will spoil by overestimation all the good of me that the first half,
by underestimation, has left intact' was not quite right; the process
of judging him is far from over, and he continues to fascinate
and intrigue.

Classified List of Works

Dates in parentheses are those of composition. The abbreviation 'fp' denotes first public performance, details of which are given where known.

Stage Works

Erwartung, Op. 17, monodrama in one act, libretto by Marie Pappenheim (1909). fp Prague, 6 June 1924

Die glückliche Hand, Op. 18, 'drama with music' in one act, libretto by A. Schoenberg (1910–13). fp Vienna, 14 October 1924

Von heute auf morgen, Op. 32, opera in one act, libretto by 'Max Blonda' [Gertrud Schoenberg] (1928–9). fp Frankfurt, 1 February 1930

Moses und Aron, opera in three acts (only acts 1 & 2 composed), libretto by A. Schoenberg (1930–2). fp 'Der Tanz um das goldene Kalb' (orchestral scene), Darmstadt, 2 July 1951; acts 1–2, concert performance, Hamburg, 12 March 1954; acts 1–2, stage performance, Zurich, 6 June 1957

Choral Works with Orchestra

Gurrelieder, oratorio (J. P. Jacobsen, trans. R. F. Arnold); solo voices, choirs and orchestra (1900–1; orchestrated 1901–3; 1910–11). fp (incomplete, first part only, with 2-piano accompaniment) Vienna, 14 January 1910; (complete) Vienna, 23 February 1913

Die Jakobsleiter, oratorio (A. Schoenberg); solo voices, choirs and orchestras (1917–22; 1944) incomplete, orchestration of the extant portion by W. Zillig. fp Vienna, 16 June 1961

Kol Nidre, Op. 39 (Jewish liturgical text, in English); speaker (male), choir, orchestra (1938). fp Los Angeles, 4 October 1938

Prelude for Mixed Chorus and Orchestra, Op. 44 (1945). fp Los Angeles, 18 November 1945

A Survivor from Warsaw, Op. 46 (A. Schoenberg); speaker (male), choir and orchestra (1947). fp Albuquerque, New Mexico, 4 November 1948

Moderner Psalm, Op. 50c (A. Schoenberg); speaker (male), choir, orchestra (1950, fragment). fp Cologne, 29 May 1956

Choral Works *a Cappella*

'Ei du Lütte' (K. Groth), (c. 1896)

'Der deutsche Michel' (O. Kernstock), (c. 1900)

Friede auf Erden, Op. 13 (C. F. Meyer) (1907), choir (1907), optional instrumental parts doubling the voices (1911). fp Vienna, 9 December 1911 (with instrumental parts)

Four Pieces, Op. 27: 'Unentrinnbar' (A. Schoenberg), 'Du sollst nicht, du musst' (A. Schoenberg), 'Mond und Menschen' (H. Bethge, after Tschan-Jo-Su), 'Der Wunsch des Liebhabers' (H. Bethge, after Hung-So-Fan), with clarinet, mandolin, violin and cello (1925)

Three Satires, Op. 28 (A. Schoenberg): 'Am Scheideweg', 'Vielseitigkeit', 'Der neue Klassicismus', with viola, cello and piano (1925)

Drei Volkslieder: 'Es gingen zwei Gespielen gut', 'Herzlieblich Lieb, durch Scheiden', 'Schein uns, du liebe Sonne' (1928–9). Other versions see *Vier deutsche Volkslieder* on page 221 and Three Folksongs, Op. 49 on page 220. fp (Nos. 2 and 3) Vienna, 10 November 1929

Six Pieces, Op. 35 (A. Schoenberg): 'Hemmung', 'Das Gesetz', 'Ausdrucksweise', 'Glück', 'Landsknechte',

'Verbundenheit' (1929–30). fp (No. 4) Berlin,
2 November 1929, (Nos. 1–3, 5, 6) Hanau,
24 October 1931

Three Folksongs, Op. 49: 'Es gingen zwei Gespielen
gut' ('Two comely maidens'); 'Der Mai tritt ein mit
Freuden' ('Now May has come with gladness'); 'Mein
Herz in steten Treuen' ('To her I shall be faithful'),
(1948). *A cappella* version of Nos. 1–3 from *Vier deutsche
Volkslieder* originally arranged for voice and piano
in 1929.

Dreimal tausend Jahre, Op. 50a (D. D. Runes), (1949).
fp Fylkingen, 29 October 1949

De profundis – 'Shir hama'alot mima'amakim' (Ps. 130
in Hebrew), Op. 50b (1950). fp Cologne, 29 January 1954

Compositions for Solo Voice and Orchestra

Six Orchestral Songs, Op. 8: 'Natur' (H. Hart),
'Das Wappenschild' (*Des Knaben Wunderhorn*),
'Sehnsucht' (*Des Knaben Wunderhorn*), 'Nie ward ich,
Herrin, müd' (Petrarch, trans. Förster), 'Voll jener
Süsse' (Petrarch, trans. Förster), 'Wenn Vöglein
klagen' (Petrarch, trans. Förster), (1903–5).
fp (Nos. 2, 5 and 6) Prague, 29 January 1914

Four Orchestral Songs, Op. 22: 'Seraphita'
(E. Dowson, trans. S. George), (1913), 'Alle welche dich
suchen' (Rilke), (1914), 'Mach mich zum Wächter
deiner Weiten' (Rilke), (1914–15), 'Vorgefühl' (Rilke),
(1916). fp Frankfurt, 21 February 1932

Compositions for Solo Voice and Instruments

Herzgewächse, Op. 20 (M. Maeterlinck, trans.
K. L. Ammer and F. von Oppeln-Bronikowski),
soprano, celesta, harp, harmonium (1911).
fp New York, 2 December 1923

Pierrot lunaire, Op. 21: *Dreimal sieben Gedichte aus
Albert Girauds Pierrot lunaire* (trans. O. E. Hartleben),
female speaker (*Sprechstimme*), flute, piccolo, clarinet,

bass clarinet, violin, viola, cello, piano (1912): Part i:
'Mondestrunken', 'Colombine', 'Der Dandy', 'Eine
blasse Wäscherin', 'Valse de Chopin', 'Madonna', 'Der
kranke Mond'; Part ii: 'Nacht', 'Gebet an Pierrot',
'Raub', 'Rote Messe', 'Galgenlied', 'Enthauptung',
'Die Kreuze'; Part iii: 'Heimweh', 'Gemeinheit',
'Parodie', 'Der Mondfleck', 'Serenade', 'Heimfahrt',
'O alter Duft'. fp Berlin, 9 (16) October 1912

Lied der Waldtaube (from *Gurrelieder*), mezzo-
soprano, 17 instruments and percussion (arr. 1922).
fp Copenhagen, 30 January 1923

Ode to Napoleon, Op. 41 (Byron), male reciter, piano,
string quartet/string orchestra (1942). fp New York,
23 November 1944

Compositions for Solo Voice and Piano

Early works: c. 32 solo songs (1893–1900)

Two Songs, Op. 1 (K. von Levetzow): 'Dank',
'Abschied' (1898). fp Vienna, 1898

Die Beiden (H. von Hofmannsthal) (1899)

Four Songs, Op. 2: 'Erwartung' (Dehmel), (1899),
'Schenk mir deinen goldenen Kamm' (Dehmel),
(1899), fp Vienna, 11 February 1904; 'Erhebung'
(Dehmel), (1899), fp Vienna, 26 January 1907;
'Waldsonne' (J. Schlaf), (c. 1900), fp Vienna,
28 April 1915

Brettl-Lieder [Cabaret songs]: 'Der genügsame
Liebhaber' (H. Salus), 'Einfältiges Lied' (Salus),
'Nachtwandler' (G. Falke), soprano, piccolo, trumpet,
side drum, piano, 'Jedem das Seine' (Colly), 'Mahnung'
(G. Hochstetter), 'Galathea' (F. Wedekind), 'Gigerlette'
(O. J. Bierbaum), 'Seit ich so viele Weiber sah'
(Aus dem *Spiegel von Arcadia*) (E. Schikaneder), (1901)

Six Songs, Op. 3: 'Wie Georg von Frundsberg
von sich selber sang' (*Des Knaben Wunderhorn*),
'Die Aufgeregten' (G. Keller), 'Warnung' (Dehmel),

'Hochzeitslied' (Jacobsen, trans. Arnold), 'Geübtes
Herz' (Keller), fp Vienna, 26 January 1907, 'Freihold'
(H. Lingg), (1899–1903), fp Vienna, 26 March 1919

Eight Songs, Op. 6: 'Traumleben' (J. Hart), fp Vienna
26 January 1907; 'Alles' (Dehmel), 'Mädchenlied'
(P. Remer), fp Vienna, 26 January 1907; 'Verlassen'
(H. Conradi), fp Vienna, 26 January 1907; 'Ghasel'
(Keller), 'Am Wegrand' (J. H. Mackay), 'Lockung'
(K. Aram), 'Der Wanderer' (F. Nietzsche), (1903–5),
fp Vienna, 28 April 1915

Two Ballads, Op. 12: 'Jane Grey' (H. Ammann),
'Der verlorene Haufen' (V. Klemperer), (1907).
fp (No. 1) Vienna, 23 October 1920

Two Songs, Op. 14: 'Ich darf nicht dankend'
(S. George), 'In diesen Wintertagen' (K. Henckel)
(1907–8). fp Vienna, 20 January 1921

Das Buch der hängenden Gärten, Op. 15 (S. George):
'Unterm Schutz von dichten Blättergründen',
'Hain in diesen Paradiesen', 'Als Neuling trat ich
ein in dein Gehege', 'Da meine Lippen reglos sind
und brennen', 'Saget mir auf welchem Pfade', 'Jedem
Werke bin ich fürder tot', 'Angst und Hoffen
wechselnd mich beklemmen', 'Wenn ich heut nicht
deinen Leib berühre', 'Streng ist uns das Glück und
Spröde', 'Das schöne Beet betracht ich mir im
Harren', 'Als wir hinter dem beblümten Tore', 'Wenn
sich bei heilger Ruh in tiefen Matten', 'Du lehnest
wider eine Silberweide', 'Sprich nicht immer von dem
Laub', 'Wir bevölkerten die abend-düstern Lauben'
(1908–9). fp Vienna, 14 January 1910

'Am Strande' (attrib. to Rilke by Schoenberg,
doubtful), (1909). Possibly intended as a part of
Op. 14. fp Hamburg, 12 January 1958

Vier deutsche Volkslieder: 'Der Mai tritt ein
mit Freuden'; 'Es gingen zwei Gespielen gut';
'Mein Herz in steten Treuen'; 'Mein Herz ist mir
gemenget' (1929–30). Nos. 1–3 arranged *a cappella*
in Three Folksongs, Op. 49 (see page 220)

Three Songs, Op. 48 (J. Haringer): 'Sommermüd',
'Tot', 'Mädchenlied' (1933). fp Los Angeles,
16 May 1950

Orchestral

Verklärte Nacht, Op. 4, arranged for string orchestra
(1917, revised 1943)

Pelleas und Melisande, Op. 5, symphonic poem,
after M. Maeterlinck (1902–3). fp Vienna,
25 January 1905

Chamber Symphony No. 1, Op. 9 (version for full
orchestra, 1922, revised 1935). fp Los Angeles,
27 December 1936

String Quartet No. 2, Op. 10 (two versions for soprano
and string orchestra, 1919 and 1929)

Five Orchestral Pieces, Op. 16: 'Vorgefühle',
'Vergangenes', 'Farben', 'Peripetie', 'Das obligate
Recitativ' (1909, version for reduced orchestra 1949).
fp London, 3 September 1912

Variations for Orchestra, Op. 31 (1926–8). fp Berlin,
2 December 1928

Begleitungsmusik zu einer Lichtspielszene, Op. 34
(1929–30). fp Frankfurt (radio), 8 April 1930

Cello Concerto, after G. M. Monn's Cembalo
Concerto in D, 1746 (1932–3). fp London,
3 February 1933 (unofficial: Antonio Sala and
Edward Clark), 7 November 1935 (official:
Emanuel Feuermann and Thomas Beecham)

Concerto for String Quartet and Orchestra, after
G. F. Handel's Concerto Grosso, Op. 6, No. 7 (1933).
fp Prague, 26 September 1934

Suite in G for string orchestra (1934). fp Los Angeles,
18 May 1935

Violin Concerto, Op. 36 (1934–6). fp Philadelphia,
6 December 1940

Chamber Symphony No. 2 (begun 1906, completed
1939). fp New York, 15 December 1940

Piano Concerto, Op. 42 (1942). fp New York,
6 February 1944

Theme and Variations for wind band, Op. 43a
(1943), version for full orchestra, Op. 43b (1943).
fp (Op. 43a) New York, 27 June 1946, (Op. 43b)
Boston 20 October 1944

Chamber Music

String Quartet in D (1897). fp (private) Vienna,
17 March 1898, (public) Vienna, 20 December 1898

Verklärte Nacht, Op. 4, after R. Dehmel, string sextet
(1899). fp Vienna, 18 March 1902

String Quartet No. 1 in D, Op. 7 (1904–5).
fp Vienna, 5 February 1907

Chamber Symphony No. 1, Op. 9, for 15 solo
instruments (1906). fp Vienna, 8 February 1907

String Quartet No. 2, Op. 10, with solo soprano
in third movement 'Litanei' and fourth movement
'Entrückung' (S. George), (1907–8). fp Vienna,
21 December 1908

Three Pieces for Chamber Orchestra (1910). fp Berlin,
10 October 1957

Die eiserne Brigade, march for piano quintet (1916)

Five Orchestral Pieces, Op. 16, arranged for
11 instruments (1920)

Serenade, Op. 24, for clarinet, bass clarinet, mandolin,
guitar, violin, viola and cello, solo bass in fourth
movement: 'O könnt' ich je der Rach' an ihr genesen'

(Petrarch, trans. K. Förster), (1920–3).
fp (private) Vienna, 2 May 1924, (public)
Donaueschingen, 2 July 1924

Weihnachtsmusik, 2 violins, cello, harmonium,
piano (1921)

Wind Quintet, Op. 26 (1923–4). fp Vienna,
13 (16) September 1924

Suite, Op. 29, for clarinets in E flat and B flat,
bass clarinet, violin, viola, cello and piano (1925–6).
fp Paris, 15 December 1927

String Quartet No. 3, Op. 30 (1927). fp Vienna,
19 September 1927

String Quartet No. 4, Op. 37 (1936). fp Los Angeles,
8 January 1937

Chamber Symphony No. 2, Op. 38 (1906–8, 1911, 1916,
1939). fp New York, 15 December 1940

String Trio, Op. 45 (1946). fp Cambridge, Mass.,
1 May 1947

Phantasy for Violin with Piano Accompaniment,
Op. 47 (1949). fp Los Angeles, 13 September 1949

**Keyboard Music (Piano, unless otherwise
indicated)**

Three Piano Pieces (1894)

Six Pieces, piano duet (1896)

Chamber Symphony No. 1, Op. 9, arranged for
piano duet, c. 1912

Three Piano Pieces, Op. 11 (1909). fp Vienna,
14 January 1910

Six Little Piano Pieces, Op. 19 (1911). fp Berlin,
4 February 1912

Five Piano Pieces, Op. 23 (1920–3). fp (Nos. 1 and 2) Vienna, 9 October 1920, (complete) Hamburg, autumn 1923

Suite for Piano, Op. 25 (1921–3). fp Vienna, 25 February 1924

Piano Piece, Op. 33a (1928–9). fp Berlin, 30 January 1931

Piano Piece, Op. 33b (1931). fp Frankfurt, 20 September 1949

Chamber Symphony No. 2, Op. 38b, arranged for piano duet (1941–2)

Variations on a Recitative for Organ, Op. 40, (1941). fp New York, 10 April 1944

Fragments and Sketches

Schoenberg left a large number of sketches and drafts, which, had they been finished, would have almost doubled his total output. Most of the sketches are brief and defy attempts to complete them. Although unfinished, the opera *Moses und Aron* and the oratorio *Die Jakobsleiter* have entered the repertoire and are listed in the appropriate sections above.

Orchestration of Other Composers' Works

Numerous operetta scores, c. 1899–1903

H. Schenker, *Vier syrische Tänze* (1903) – lost. fp Berlin, 5 November 1903

L. van Beethoven, 'Adelaide', Op. 46; C. Loewe, 'Der Nöck', Op. 129; F. Schubert, *Drei Lieder* (1912); orchestration of piano accompaniment, prepared for the soprano Julia Culp

J. S. Bach, Chorale Prelude 'Komm, Gott, Schöpfer, heiliger Geist', BWV 667 (1922). fp New York, 7 December 1922

J. S. Bach, Chorale Prelude 'Schmücke dich, O liebe Seele', BWV 654 (1922). fp New York, 7 December 1922

J. S. Bach, Prelude and Fugue in E flat, BWV 552 (1928). fp Berlin, 10 November 1929 (Furtwängler); Vienna, 11 November 1929 (Webern)

J. Brahms, Piano Quartet in G, Op. 25 (1937). fp Los Angeles, 7 May 1938

Continuo realizations in G. M. Monn's Sinfonia, Divertimento and Concertos for the series *Denkmäler der Musik in Österreich* (vol. 39, 1911–12), and F. S. I. A. Tůma's Partitas and Symphony

Arrangements (Reductions) for Small Ensemble of Other Composers' Works

G. Mahler, *Lieder eines fahrenden Gesellen* (1920). fp Vienna, 6 February 1920

M. Reger, *Eine romantische Suite*, Op. 125 (1919–20, with R. Kolisch)

G. Mahler, *Das Lied von der Erde* (1921). fp July 1983

J. Sioly, *Weil i a alter Drahrer bin* (1921)

J. Strauss, *Rosen aus dem Süden* (1921)

J. Strauss, *Lagunen-Walzer* (1921)

J. Strauss, *Kaiser-Walzer* (1925?). fp Barcelona, 26 April 1925

Canons

Between 1905 and 1949 Schoenberg wrote close to forty brief contrapuntal compositions, mostly based on some intricate scheme, requiring resolution according to a rule (*canon*) worded cryptically. These compositions were intended as greetings and gifts to friends and pupils (dedicatees include

David Josef Bach, Erwin Stein, the Amsterdam
Concertgebouw Orchestra, Alban Berg, G. B. Shaw
and Thomas Mann) and, although they contain
wonderful examples of ingenuity and technical
mastery, most of them were not intended for
public performance. Possible exceptions are
the three canons that Schoenberg appended to
the Three Satires, Op. 28.

Literary Works and Diaries

Texte (Vienna, 1926, reprinted Vienna, n.d.).
Includes texts for *Die glückliche Hand*,
Totentanz der Principien, *Die Jakobsleiter* and
the poem Requiem.

Der biblische Weg, drama (1926–7)

*Psalmen, Gebete und andere Gespräche mit und über
Gott* (Mainz, 1956)

Leggere il cielo. Diari 1912, 1914, 1923, edited by
Anna Maria Morazzoni (Milan, 1999). The Italian
edition brings together Schoenberg's fragmentary
diaries; their English versions are available only in
various periodical publications.

Theoretical Works

Harmonielehre (Vienna, 1911, revised edition, 1922);
English editions: *Harmony* (1948, abridged version),
Theory of Harmony (London, 1978). A systematic
re-examination of Western harmonic theory
from Bach to early Schoenberg, one of
the fundamental theoretical works of the
twentieth century.

*Coherence, Counterpoint, Instrumentation, Instruction
in Form* (1917, 1926), edited by S. Neff and translated
by C. M. Cross (Lincoln, Nebraska, 1994)

*The Musical Idea and the Logic, Technique and Art
of its Presentation* (1934–6), edited and translated by
P. Carpenter and S. Neff (New York, 1995)

Pedagogical Works

Models for Beginners in Composition (Los Angeles, 1942)

Structural Functions of Harmony (1948), edited by
H. Searle (London, 1954), and L. Stein (revised
edition, New York, 1969)

Preliminary Exercises in Counterpoint (1936–50),
edited by L. Stein (London, 1963)

Fundamentals of Musical Composition (1937–48),
edited by G. Strang and L. Stein (London 1967)

Essays and Correspondence

Style and Idea, edited by D. Newlin (New York, 1950);
second, considerably extended edition, edited by
L. Stein (London, 1975). The extended version includes
all of Schoenberg's major essays and a large number
of critical and polemical articles.

Letters, edited by E. Stein, (trans.) Eithne Wilkins
and Ernst Kaiser (London, 1964). An enlarged
version of the German original (Mainz, 1958), often
carelessly translated.

Gesammelte Schriften, vol. i, edited by I. Vojtěch
(Frankfurt, 1976). Intended as a definitive edition of
all of Schoenberg's extant writings.

*Arnold Schoenberg/Wassily Kandinsky. Letters,
Pictures and Documents*, edited by Jelena Hahl-Koch
and translated by J. C. Crawford (London, 1984)

The Berg-Schoenberg Correspondence: Selected Letters,
edited by J. Brand, C. Hailey and D. Harris
(New York, 1987)

*Arnold Schoenberg Correspondence. A Collection of
Translated and Annotated Letters Exchanged with
Guido Adler, Pablo Casals, Emanuel Feuermann and
Olin Downes*, edited by Egbert M. Ennulat
(Metuchen, NJ and London, 1991)

Arnold Schönberg / Thomas Mann, A proposito del Doctor Faustus. Lettere 1930–1951, translated by Fernanda Mancini and Gabrio Taglietti (Milan, 1993). French edition: *Arnold Schönberg / Thomas Mann, A propos du Docteur Faustus. Lettres 1930–1951* (Lausanne, 2002). German edition, with additional material: *Apropos Doktor Faustus: Briefwechsel Arnold Schönberg – Thomas Mann 1930–1951*, edited by E. Randol Schoenberg (Vienna, 2008 [2009])

Alexander Zemlinsky, Briefwechsel der Wiener Schule: Briefwechsel mit Arnold Schönberg, Anton Webern, Alban Berg und Franz Schreker, edited by Horst Weber (Darmstadt, 1995)

Stile herrschen, Gedanken siegen: Ausgewählte Schriften, edited by Anna Maria Morazzoni, Petra Eisenhardt and Nuria Schoenberg-Nono (Mainz, 2007). An anthology with the essays published in the languages of their first appearance in print (German and English).

Further Reading

Originally intended for his students at the University
of California, Los Angeles, Schoenberg's textbooks
(listed on page 224 under the titles Theoretical Works
and Pedagogical Works) have been used by generations
of music students, especially in the English-speaking
world. Apart from his theoretical and pedagogical
works, Schoenberg published a large number of essays
as well as critical and polemical articles. He was also
a prolific letter writer, and selected letters from his
correspondence with Alban Berg, Wassily Kandinsky
and Thomas Mann, among others, have been published
over the years, as listed in the previous pages. However,
a new, complete, edition of Schoenberg's letters is badly
needed, as only a small number of letters is included in
the collection published in German in 1958. In a number
of instances the editor, Erwin Stein, omitted portions
of text containing personal remarks about people still
alive at the time of publication. *Letters* (London, 1964)
is an enlarged version of the German original, but
often carelessly translated. Many important biog-
raphies and critical studies on Schoenberg and his
work are available only in German. Several recent
titles are listed here.

Adorno, T. W. *Philosophy of New Music*, translated
and edited by R. Hullot-Kentor (Minneapolis,
University of Minnesota Press, 2006). This translation
from the original German (*Philosophie der neuen
Musik*, Tübingen, 1949) supersedes an earlier version
(*Philosophy of Modern Music*, translated by Mitchell
and Bloomster) in its accuracy, but is still wanting in
places. A seminal, if controversial, work; very widely
read in the past few decades.

Auner, J. (ed.) *A Schoenberg Reader. Documents of
a Life* (New Haven and London, Yale University Press,
2003). An extensive annotated collection of excerpts

from Schoenberg's writings, in chronological order,
charting the development of his ideas and his
relationship to the society in which he lived.

Freitag, E. *Arnold Schönberg in Selbstzeugnissen
und Bilddokumenten* (Reinbek bei Hamburg,
Rowohlt, 1973). An illustrated concise biography,
with quotations from documentary sources.

Frisch, W. (ed.) *Schoenberg and his World*
(Princeton University Press, 1999). An illuminating
selection of original documents and critical essays,
covering a long period from c. 1912 to the present day.

Gervink, M. *Arnold Schönberg und seine Zeit*
(Laaber-Verlag, Laaber, 2000). A life-and-works
study, well proportioned and informative. Extensive
references to primary sources.

Haimo, E. *Schoenberg's Serial Odyssey: the Evolution
of his Twelve-Tone Method, 1914–1928* (Oxford,
Clarendon Presss 1990). A guide to the technical
aspects of Schoenberg's innovative system.

Henke, M. *Arnold Schönberg* (Munich, Deutscher
Taschenbuch-Verlag, 2001). An introduction to the
composer and his time, intended for general
readership, in its scope close to the present volume.

Hollein, M. and B. Perica (eds.) *Die Visionen
des Arnold Schönberg. Jahre der Malerei/The Visions
of Arnold Schönberg. The Painting Years* (Ostfildern-
Ruit, Hatje Cantz, 2002). A bilingual, German-English
edition of essays on Schoenberg the painter and an
illustrated catalogue of his paintings, drawings and
sketches. Published on the occasion of an exhibition
held at the Schirn Kunsthalle, Frankfurt, 2002.

Krones, H. *Arnold Schönberg. Werk und Leben*
(Vienna, Steinbauer Verlag, 2005). A well-balanced
study in clear and readable German. The first
three chapters cover the chronology and discuss
a representative sample of his European and American
works; the following three chapters ('Foundations of

Schoenberg's Thought', 'Schoenberg as a Teacher and Theorist', and 'Aspects of Schoenberg's Personality') offer a comprehensive critical survey.

Macdonald, M. *Schoenberg* (London, Dent, 1976, revised edition, Oxford University Press, 2008), (*Master Musicians* series). A life-and-works survey, now revised in the light of new research.

Meyer, Ch. and Muxender, T. (eds.) *Arnold Schönberg. Catalogue raisonné*, 2 vols. (Vienna, Arnold Schönberg Center, 2005). A detailed catalogue of Schoenberg's paintings, drawings, sketches and designs.

Newlin, D. *Bruckner, Mahler, Schoenberg* (New York, Norton, 1947). The first attempt to place Schoenberg into a full historical context of music in Vienna; written by a former student.

— *Schoenberg Remembered: Diaries and Recollections (1938–76)* (New York, Pendragon Press 1980). A fascinating first-hand account of Schoenberg as a teacher.

Payne, A. *Schoenberg* (Oxford University Press, 1968). A concise introduction to the works and compositional technique.

Reich, W. *Schoenberg, a Critical Biography* (London, Longman, 1971). Translation from the German (*Schönberg, oder der konservative Revolutionär*, 1968), more biographical detail than in Stuckenschmidt (1959), less on the technical aspects of the music.

Ringer, A. *Arnold Schoenberg: the Composer as Jew* (Oxford, Clarendon Press 1990). A sensitive and persuasive account of Schoenberg's relationship to Judaism and his exposure to racial prejudice.

Arnold Schönberg. Das Leben im Werk (Stuttgart-Weimar-Kassel, Metzler, 2002). Explores compositional, psychological, cultural and political aspects of Schoenberg's work.

Rosen, C. *Schoenberg* (London, Marion Boyars, 1975), (*Fontana Modern Masters* series). A brief but very perceptive introduction to Schoenberg's music, ideas and techniques of composition.

Schoenberg-Nono, N. *Arnold Schoenberg, 1874–1951. Lebensgeschichte in Begegnungen* (Klagenfurt, Ritter Verlag, 1992). An account of Schoenberg's life presented through photographs, facsimiles and documents, compiled by the composer's daughter.

Stuckenschmidt, H. H. *Arnold Schoenberg*, translated by E. Temple Roberts and H. Searle (New York, Grove Press, 1959). Translation of a German original (Zurich, Atlantis Verlag, 1951, revised 1957). A brief life-and-works monograph, intended as an introduction to the composer.

Arnold Schoenberg, His Life, World and Work, translated by H. Searle (London, Calder, 1977). Translation of a German original (Zurich, Atlantis Verlag, 1974). The only detailed biography in English. An ambitious study but marred by unclear presentation and numerous inaccuracies.

Wellesz, E. *Arnold Schoenberg* (London, Dent, 1925, reprinted, with new material, London, Galliard, 1971). Originally published in German in 1921; an important document of critical understanding by a former pupil who had a difficult relationship with his teacher.

Selective Discography

For a composer whose music is, allegedly, not popular, Schoenberg has been very well represented in recordings. The first recordings of some of his piano music and of *Verklärte Nacht* date from the 1920s. New technical advances in sound recording as well as Schoenberg's presence in California in the 1930s and 1940s encouraged several expatriate Austrian and German interpreters to embark on ambitious projects, benefiting from Schoenberg's criticism and advice. Thus in 1936 and 1937 Kolisch's quartet recorded the complete String Quartets and in 1940 Erika Stiedry-Wagner recorded *Pierrot lunaire* with an ensemble conducted by the composer. These and various subsequent recordings featuring the musicians closely associated with Schoenberg have been listed below as historical. Most of these date from the 1950s, and already belong to the era of the modern LP record.

Although most of Schoenberg's works can be found on CD, the recording industry gives significant preference to Schoenberg's early tonal works. The recordings of *Verklärte Nacht*, *Gurrelieder* and *Pelleas und Melisande* are too numerous to list and in some cases it would be invidious to single out a particular disc as the best version available. The list that follows has been compiled with the aim of offering a variety of performances and performing attitudes. Schoenberg encompassed late Romanticism and Modernism and his aesthetic belief singled out 'expression' as an important factor. The elusive concept of 'expression' underwent a significant change, not only during the 1920s, but much more profoundly after World War II, when the new generation of composer-performers, headed by Pierre Boulez and Karlheinz Stockhausen, sought to free the act of interpretation from subjective elements, aiming at a clear representation of the structure of a musical work while eschewing the allegedly Romantic freedom and emotion. This is in itself a declaration of their ideas of what the emotional impact of the music should be and thus the 'emotion' is not removed, but only given a new meaning.

Pierre Boulez and Robert Craft have been assiduous in recording Schoenberg's music and the list would be shorter and more user-friendly if it was limited to their recordings. Instead, the choice has been made in order to show different approaches. It is likely that Alfred Brendel's version of the Piano Concerto, conducted by Rafael Kubelik, is closer to Schoenberg's idea of the work, rooted as it is in the tradition of the great pianists of the early part of the twentieth century. On the other hand, Mitsuko Uchida's recording, conducted by Boulez, is a good example of a more modern approach, stressing the crispness of the piano part and of the orchestral texture.

Any list of recordings is bound to become obsolete quickly, but various websites facilitate the purchase of recordings otherwise considered no longer commercially available.

Historical

The Four String Quartets
A reissue of the recordings made by the Kolisch Quartet in 1936–7 under Schoenberg's supervision. Includes spoken commentaries by Schoenberg and members of the Quartet
ARCHIPHON 2 CD ARC-103/04

Pierrot lunaire
Erika Stiedry-Wagner (voice), Leonard Posella (flute and piccolo), Kalman Bloch (clarinet and bass clarinet), Rudolf Kolisch (violin and viola), Stefan Auber (cello), Eduard Steuermann (piano); conducted by Arnold Schoenberg. Recorded in Los Angeles, 24 September 1940. With Trio, Op. 45
CBS CD MPK 45695

Ode to Napoleon
Mack Harrell (voice), Eduard Steuermann (piano), New York Philharmonic. Live recording of the first performance, conducted by Artur Rodzinsky.

With E. Bloch, *Shelomo* and D. Shostakovich,
Symphony No. 5
AS Disc CD ASD 631

String Trio, Op. 45
Koldofsky Trio: Adolf Koldofsky (violin),
Cecil Figelski (viola), George Neikrug (cello).
Recorded c. 1953
Classic CD C6172

Violin Concerto
Louis Krasner (violin); West German Radio
Orchestra, Cologne, conducted by Dimitri
Mitropoulos. Recorded live, Cologne, 16 July 1954
GM Recordings CD GM2006CD

Moses und Aron
Various performers including Hans Herbert Fiedler,
Helmut Krebs, Ilona Steingruber-Wildgans, Ursula
Zollenkops. Chorus of the Hamburg Academy of
Music, Chorus and Orchestra of North German
Radio, conducted by Hans Rosbaud. Recorded
broadcast by Norddeutscher Rundfunk, Hamburg,
12 March 1954
CBS LP 78213

Complete piano music
Eduard Steuermann (piano)
Columbia LP ML 5216

Stage Works

Erwartung
Phyllis Bryn-Julson, City of Birmingham Symphony
Orchestra, conducted by Simon Rattle. With Chamber
Symphony No. 1, Op. 9, Variations for Orchestra, Op. 31
EMI Classics CD 555212-2

Die glückliche Hand
John Bröcheler (baritone); SWR Sinfonieorchester
Baden-Baden und Freiburg; Rundfunkchor Berlin;
conducted by Michael Gielen. With Berg, *Der Wein*,
Webern, Five Orchestral Pieces, Op. 16, Cantata,
Op. 29, Steuermann, Variations for Orchestra, Op. 31

and Gielen, *Pflicht und Neigung*
Hänssler Classic CD 93080

Von heute auf morgen
Christine Whittlesey, Claudia Barainsky, Ryszard
Karczykowski, Richard Salter, Annabelle Hahn,
Radio-Sinfonie-Orchester Frankfurt, conducted by
Michael Gielen
CPO CD 999 532-2

Moses und Aron
Various performers including David Pittman-
Jennings, Chris Merritt, Gabriele Fontana, László
Polgár, Yvonne Naef, John Graham Hall; Chorus of
Nederlandse Opera, Zaans Jongenskoor, Jongens
Muziekschool Waterland, Royal Concertgebouw
Orchestra; conducted by Pierre Boulez
Deutsche Grammophon CD 449 174-2GH2, 2 CDs

**Works for Soloists, Choir and Orchestra or
Instrumental Ensemble**

Gurrelieder
Karita Mattila, Anne Sofie von Otter, Thomas Moser,
Philip Langridge, Thomas Quasthoff; Rundfunkchor
Berlin, MDR Rundfunkchor, Leipzig, Ernst Senff
Chor, Berlin, Berlin Philharmonic; conducted by
Simon Rattle
EMI Classics CD 586501-2, 2 CDs

Die Jakobsleiter
Dietrich Henschel, Salomé Kammer, Heidi Meier,
Jonas Kaufmann, Stephan Rügamer, Kurt Azesberger,
Michael Volle, James Johnson; Rundfunkchor Berlin,
Deutsches-Symphonie-Orchester, Berlin; conducted
by Kent Nagano. With *Friede auf Erden*
Harmonia Mundi CD HMC 801821

Kol Nidre
James Johnson (voice), Rundfunkchor, Berlin, SWR
Radio-Sinfonieorchester Baden-Baden and Freiburg,
conducted by Michael Gielen. With Kurtág, *Stele* and
Mahler, Symphony No. 2
Hänssler Classic CD 93001, 2 CDs

A Survivor from Warsaw
John Tomlinson (speaker), Chor der Sächsischen
Staatsoper, Staatskapelle Dresden, conducted by
Giuseppe Sinopoli. With Six Songs with Orchestral
Accompaniment, Op. 8, Chamber Symphony No. 1
and *Begleitungsmusik zu einer Lichtspielszene*
TELDEC 3984-22905-2

Six Songs with Orchestral Accompaniment, Op. 8
Alessandra Marc (voice).
See *A Survivor from Warsaw*, above

Four Orchestral Songs, Op. 22
Chamber Symphony No. 1, Op. 9
Variations for Orchestra, Op. 31
Catherine Wyn-Rogers (mezzo-soprano),
Philharmonia Orchestra; conducted by Robert Craft.
With Bach orchestrations: 'Schmücke dich, o liebe
Seele', 'Komm, Gott, Schöpfer, heiliger Geist',
Prelude and fugue in E flat (St Anne)
KOCH INTERNATIONAL CLASSICS CD 37463-2

Orchestral Music

Verklärte Nacht
Chamber Symphony No. 1, Op. 9
Variations for Orchestra, Op. 31
Five Orchestral Pieces, Op. 16
Six Songs with Orchestral Accompaniment, Op. 8
Erwartung
Anja Silja, Los Angeles Philharmonic Orchestra,
conducted by Zubin Mehta; Vienna Philharmonic
Orchestra, Cleveland Orchestra, conducted by
Christoph von Dohnanyi
DECCA CD 448 279-2 DF2, 2 CDs

Pelleas und Melisande, Op. 5
Variations for Orchestra, Op. 31
Chicago Symphony Orchestra, conducted by
Pierre Boulez
ERATO CD 2292-45827-2

Chamber Symphonies Nos. 1 and 2
Verklärte Nacht (string orchestra version)

Chamber Orchestra of Europe, conducted by
Heinz Holliger
TELDEC CD 0927 44399 2

Begleitungsmusik zu einer Lichtspielszene
Verklärte Nacht
Chamber Symphony No. 2
Chamber Orchestra of Europe, conducted
by Heinz Holliger
TELDEC CD 9031-77314-2

Concertos

Concerto for Violin and Orchestra
Hilary Hahn, Swedish Radio Symphony Orchestra,
conducted by Esa-Pekka Salonen. With Sibelius,
Violin Concerto
DEUTSCHE GRAMMOPHON CD 477 7346

Concerto for Violin and Orchestra
Zvi Zeitlin, Bavarian Radio Symphony Orchestra,
conducted by Rafael Kubelik. With Schoenberg,
Piano Concerto (A. Brendel) and Berg, Violin
Concerto (H. Szeryng)
DEUTSCHE GRAMMOPHON CD 469 606-2

Concerto for Piano and Orchestra
Mitsuko Uchida, Cleveland Orchestra, conducted by
Pierre Boulez. With Schoenberg, Piano Pieces, Op. 11
and Op. 19, Berg, Sonata, Op. 1 and Webern,
Variations, Op. 27
PHILIPS CD 468-033-2

Chamber Music

Quartet in D-major (1897)
String Quartets Nos. 1–4
Verklärte Nacht, Op. 4
Chamber Symphony No. 1, Op. 9 (arr. Webern),
Six Little Piano Pieces, Op. 19 (arr. Guittart)
Quintet, Op. 26
String Trio, Op. 45
Phantasy for Violin with Piano Accompaniment, Op. 47
Ode to Napoleon

Concerto for String Quartet after Handel
Schoenberg Quartet (Janneke van der Meer, violin;
Wim de Jong, violin; Henk Guittart, viola; Viola de
Hoog, cello), Susan Narucki, J. E. van Regteren, Taco
Kooistra, Sepp Grotenhuis, Michael Grandage,
Arnhem Philharmonic Orchestra, conducted
by Roberto Benzi
CHANDOS CD CHAN 9939

String Quartets Nos. 1–4
New Vienna String Quartet, Evelyn Lear (soprano)
PHILIPS CD 464 046-2-PM2

Pierrot lunaire
Chamber Symphony No. 1, Op. 9, in A
Marianne Pousseur, Ensemble Musique Oblique,
conducted by Philippe Herreweghe.
HARMONIA MUNDI CD HMA 195 1390

Pierrot lunaire
Jane Manning, Nash Ensemble, conducted by
Simon Rattle. With Webern, Concerto, Op. 24
CHANDOS CD 6543

Herzgewächse, Op. 20
Five Orchestral Pieces, Op. 16
A Survivor from Warsaw
Serenade, Op. 24
Eileen Hulse (soprano), London Symphony Orchestra,
conducted by Robert Craft, with Simon Callow
(speaker) and Stephen Varcoe (baritone)
KOCH INTERNATIONAL CLASSICS CD 3-7263-2H1

Quintet for Wind Instruments, Op. 26
Danzi Quintet. With H. Eisler,
Divertimento, Op. 4 and *Vierzehn Arten*
der Regen zu beschreiben, Op. 70
BERLIN CLASSICS CD 0092552BC

Serenade, Op. 24
Suite, Op. 29
Stephen Varcoe (baritone), 20th-Century Classics
Ensemble, conducted by Robert Craft
KOCH INTERNATIONAL CLASSICS CD 3-7334-2

Serenade, Op. 24
Five Orchestral Pieces, Op. 16
Ode to Napoleon
John Shirley-Quirk (*Serenade*), David Wilson-Johnson
(*Ode*). Members of the Ensemble Intercontemporain.
BBC Symphony Orchestra, conducted by
Pierre Boulez
SONY CD SMK 48463

Suite, Op. 29
Verklärte Nacht (string sextet version)
Three Pieces for Chamber Orchestra (unpublished
sketches from 1910)
Members of the Ensemble Intercontemporain,
BBC Symphony Orchestra, conducted by
Pierre Boulez
SONY CD SMK 48 465

String Trio, Op. 45
Phantasy for Violin with Piano Accompaniment, Op. 47
Stück (early work)
Gidon Kremer (violin), members of the Kremerata
Musica. With Berg, *Adagio* from the *Kammerkonzert*,
Vier Stücke für Klarinette und Klavier, Op. 5;
Mahler, *Piano Quartet* (1876); Webern, *Drei kleine*
Stücke für Violoncello und Klavier, Op. 11,
Zwei Stücke für Violoncello und Klavier (1899),
Vier Stücke für Violine und Klavier, Op. 7,
Violoncello sonata (1914)
DEUTSCHE GRAMMOPHON CD 447 112-2 GH

Solo Songs with Piano Accompaniment

Brettl-Lieder [Cabaret songs]
Four Songs, Op. 2
Six Songs, Op. 3
Eight Songs, Op. 6
Songs, Op. Posth.
Two Ballads, Op. 12
Two Songs, Op. 14
Deutsche Volkslieder (1928–9)
Mitsuko Shirai (mezzo-soprano),
Hartmut Höll (piano)
CAPRICCIO CD 10514

Piano and Organ Music

Piano Concerto, Op. 42
Three Piano Pieces, Op. 11
Six Little Piano Pieces, Op. 19
Five Piano Pieces, Op. 23
Piano Pieces, Op. 33a and b
Suite for Piano, Op. 25
Maurizio Pollini (piano), Berlin Philharmonic
Orchestra, conducted by Claudio Abbado.
With Webern, Variations, Op. 27
DEUTSCHE GRAMMOPHON CD 471 361-2 GPE

Three Piano Pieces, Op. 11
Six Little Piano Pieces, Op. 19
Five Piano Pieces, Op. 23
Suite for Piano, Op. 25
Piano Pieces, Op. 33a and b
Peter Hill (piano).
With Berg, Sonata, Op. 1
and Webern, Variations, Op. 27
NAXOS CD 8553870

Variations on a Recitative for Organ, Op. 40
Sonata for organ (fragment)
Hans-Ola Ericsson (organ).
With Frescobaldi, *Ricercare cromatico*
and Ligeti, *Ricercare,*
Zwei Etüden, Volumina
BIS CD 509

Choral Music

Friede auf Erden, Op. 13
Four Pieces, Op. 27
Three Satires, Op. 28
Six Pieces, Op. 35
Kol Nidre
A Survivor from Warsaw
Three Folksongs, Op. 49
Dreimal tausend Jahre, Op. 50a
De profundis, Op. 50b
Modern Psalm, Op. 50c
Drei Volksliedsätze

Two early choral settings (1905)
John Shirley-Quirk (voice), BBC Chorus,
BBC Symphony Orchestra, conducted by
Pierre Boulez
SONY CLASSICAL SM2K 44571, 2 CDs

Three Satires, Op. 28
Four Pieces, Op. 27
Six Pieces, Op. 35
Three Folksongs, Op. 49
Friede auf Erden, Op. 13
Dreimal tausend Jahre, Op. 50a
Psalm 130, Op. 50b
Südfunk-Chor, Stuttgart, conducted by Rupert Huber
ARTE NOVA CLASSICS CD 74321 27799 2

Friede auf Erden, Op. 13
Drei Volksliedsätze
Verbundenheit, Op. 35, No. 6
Dreimal tausend Jahre, Op. 50a
De profundis, Op. 50b
Chamber Symphony No. 1, Op. 9
Choeur de chambre Accentus, Ensemble
Intercontemporain, conducted by Laurence Equilbey
and Jonathan Nott (Chamber Symphony)
NAÏVE CD V 5008

Miscellaneous Pieces from the American Period

Suite for String Orchestra in G
Chamber Symphony No. 2
Theme and Variations, Op. 43b
Deutsche Symphonie-Orchester, Berlin, conducted
by John Mauceri
DECCA CD 448 619-2DH

Transcriptions and Arrangements

Concerto for String Quartet and Orchestra (adapted
from Handel)
Lied der Waldtaube (from *Gurrelieder*)
Das Buch der hängenden Gärten
Suite for Piano, Op. 25
Fred Sherry String Quartet, 20th-Century Classics

Ensemble, Jennifer Lane, Christopher Oldfather,
conducted by Robert Craft
Naxos CD 8.557520

Reger, *Eine romantische Suite*, Op. 125
J. Strauss, *Kaiser-Walzer*
Rosen aus dem Süden
J. Sioly, *Weil i a alter Drahrer bin*
F. Schubert, *Ständchen*
L. Denza, *Funiculì – Funiculà*
Marcus Schäfer, soloists of the Opéra National
de Lyon
Elatus CD 0927-49552-2

Concerto for violoncello and orchestra, after Monn's
Concerto in D major for harpsichord
Yo-Yo Ma, cello, Boston Symphony Orchestra,
conducted by Seiji Ozawa. With R. Strauss,
Don Quixote
CBS CD MK 39863

Five Orchestral Pieces, Op. 16 (arr. Greissle)
Die glückliche Hand, Op. 18 (arr. Tuercke)
Variations on a Recitative for Organ, Op. 40
(arr. Greissle)
J. Strauss, *Kaiser-Walzer* (arr. Schoenberg)
Jörg Gottschick (baritone), Ensemble United Berlin
and United Voices, conducted by Peter Hirsch. In
addition to Schoenberg's arrangement of a popular
Strauss waltz, this CD contains an intriguing
collection of Schoenberg's music originally written
for very large performing forces or for organ, here
arranged for small ensemble. The arrangements
continue in the tradition started by Schoenberg
and his associates for the concerts of the Verein für
private Musikaufführungen (Society for Private
Musical Performances).
Ars Musici CD AM 1344-2

Index

Page numbers in italics refer to picture captions